BRUCE RIEDER

D0287728

# PRAISE FOR *FROM REBEL YELL TO REVOLUTION*

"*From Rebel Yell to Revolution* must surely be the richest, most detailed accounting of the complex period when the 'Old U' transitioned to the 'New U.' So far as I know, no one else has written so honestly and completely on life inside the University during this period. Joel Gardner's book is full of wonderful anecdotes – road trips and big weekends, the night when Jerry Rubin and William Kunstler spoke, et al – each mined for evidence of what the University became in his time, and what it did not. Gardner's experiences make the book hum, and his sharp eye for significance in every scene makes the book memorable. We, his readers, and fellow alumni, are fortunate to have it."

—John T. Casteen III
   President, University of Virginia, 1990-2010


"Joel Gardner came to the University of Virginia at a time of great upheaval in the nation, and he watched it unfold and affect UVA from 1966 to 1970. UVA had long been more a place of social rest than unrest, but all that changed during Gardner's years in Charlottesville. How could it not? The civil rights movement, the anti-Vietnam War protests, and locally, a weakening of the stranglehold fraternities had had on student life, the beginnings of coeducation, and the death of the coat-and-tie tradition (and many other traditions, too) all transformed the University in record time.

Gardner gives us the special perspective and insight of a keen observer and participant on-the-ground (or Grounds, as the campus is called at UVA). This book will bring back many memories, good and bad, for those who were at the University in the late 1960s. It will also help those who have attended the college since that time understand how we got to the present. And for historians and sociologists, Gardner presents a fascinating case study of a noted community that quickly underwent massive shifts, yet survived and thrived."

—Dr. Larry J. Sabato
   Director, Center for Politics and University Professor of Politics
   University of Virginia

"If you have a love for the University of Virginia, you should read this book. If you want to understand how universities have evolved over the past fifty years, you should read this book. Joel Gardner, UVA class of '70, has written a bildungsroman of his UVA days which spanned the society-altering year of 1968. When Gardner arrived at UVA in 1966, he and the university were part of America's traditional conservative stock. Four years later, the university and our country had changed. For universities, that change continues to this day. For those puzzled or appalled by the radicalization of universities in America, read Gardner's book to better understand where and when those changes began. For those of you who think change has not yet gone far enough, read Gardner's book to better understand the historical antecedents of today's modern elite university. The story is compelling, the facts are intriguing, and it is spectacularly well-written to boot."

—Allan C. Stam
    Dean and Professor, Frank Batten School of Leadership and Public Policy
    University of Virginia

"*From Rebel Yell to Revolution* is both a compelling personal memoir and a captivating history of higher education during four years of upheaval and tumult... Gardner's book is engaging and thought provoking - a must-read not only for any and all graduates of the University of Virginia, who will find it informative and endearing, but for anyone interested in higher education in America."

—Kenneth G. Elzinga
    Robert C. Taylor Professor of Economics
    University of Virginia

# FROM REBEL YELL TO REVOLUTION

## My Four Years at UVA 1966-1970

# FROM REBEL YELL TO REVOLUTION

My Four Years at UVA 1966-1970

Joel B. Gardner

Brandylane
PUBLISHERS OF BOOKS SINCE 1985

Copyright 2018 by Joel B. Gardner. No part of this book may be reproduced in any form or by any electronic or mechanical means, or the facilitation thereof, including information storage and retrieval systems, without permission in writing from the publisher, except in the case of brief quotations published in articles and reviews. Any educational institution wishing to photocopy part or all of the work for classroom use, or individual researchers who would like to obtain permission to reprint the work for educational purposes, should contact the publisher.

ISBN: 978-1-947860-03-2

LCCN: 2018932251

front cover image, left, courtesy of *Corks and Curls*
front cover image, right, courtesy of *UVA Special Collections*
back cover image, courtesy of *Corks and Curls*
cover design by Michael Hardison

*To better preserve the authenticity and unique spirit of the time and place reflected in this text, the publisher has elected to follow University of Virginia style conventions in the capitalization of select terms and phrases.*

First Edition
Printed in the United States

Published by Brandylane Publishers, Inc

PUBLISHERS OF BOOKS / SINCE 1985

*This book is dedicated to the memory of my beloved parents*

A. Alfred and Shirley Gardner

*My parents at my graduation, 1970*

*"Character Above All"*

# —TABLE OF CONTENTS—

Introduction     *1*

Prologue     *5*

## —FIRST YEAR—
## THE OLD U
### *1966-1967*

The Journey Begins     *13*

McCormick Road     *15*

Introducing the Class of 1970     *19*

Orientation     *23*

Coats and Ties     *26*

Rings, Ribbons, and Sevens     *30*

There Is No Degree of Honor     *35*

The Lawn     *43*

Don't Go Up to the Balcony     *45*

Down the Road     *46*

The Largest Open Distillery in the Country     *52*

The Hair Fair     *56*

Rush     *58*

Big Weekends     *65*

Dean Runk     *75*

Pledging     *78*

The Halls of Academia     *86*

A Hint of Coeducation     *88*

"Hoot" Gibson Fires a Blank                                      89

The Charlottesville Bubble                                       91

Wahoo Forever                                                    92

## —SECOND YEAR—
## CRACKS IN THE FOUNDATION
### *1967-1968*

Introduction                                                     97

Back to McCormick Road                                           98

Brotherhood                                                      101

Expanding Horizons                                               103

They Paved Paradise and Put Up a Parking Lot                     105

In the Classroom with Two Giants                                 107

The Bubble Deflates                                              110

"Shitty" Is Dead                                                 114

The Fraternities Falter                                          115

## —THIRD YEAR—
## THE BUBBLE BURSTS
### *1968-1969*

Introduction                                                     123

Change Is in the Air                                             124

UVA's "Rosa Parks" Moment                                        129

UVA's "Monty Python" Moment                                      131

Two More Legends in the Classroom                                133

Election Night                                                   135

I Toss My Hat in the Ring                                        137

The Bubble Bursts                                 141

The Night They Drove Old Dixie Down               151

An Unsettling Sesquicentennial                    152

Boot the Hoot                                     155

An Unwelcome "Welcome"                            157

Not Just Another Election                         159

The End of Innocence                              163

—FOURTH YEAR—
REVOLUTION
*1969-1970*

Introduction                                      171

The Crackerbox                                    172

Counterculture Meets Cavalier Culture             175

The War Takes Center Stage                        177

What Are You Afraid Of?                           182

The Birth of the Jefferson Party                  184

A Barrier is Broken                               188

A Night to Remember                               189

The Calm Before the Storm                         191

The Fuse Is Lit                                   194

Revolution                                        202

What a Long Strange Trip It's Been                223


Epilogue                                          225

About the Author                                  229

Photo Credits                                     231

# INTRODUCTION

To paraphrase Ben Hecht's opening lines in the classic film of the Old South, Gone with the Wind: There was a land of Cavaliers and tradition called the Old U. Here, in this pretty world, the coat and tie took its last bow. It was a land of party weekends and bourbon; road trips, rings and ribbons; where camaraderie trumped causes, cordiality bested confrontation, and fraternities ruled the roost. Look for it only in books, for it is no more than a dream remembered, a culture gone with the wind…

Well, that was the world that I entered when I arrived at the University of Virginia from New York City in 1966, a total and complete stranger to that way of life. At that time, UVA was a tradition-bound, relatively small, all-men's school ensconced in the sleepy central Virginia town of Charlottesville amidst the splendor of Thomas Jefferson's neoclassical masterpiece. It was a school where little had changed in decades and where a student from the 1950s or even the 1920s would have felt right at home. Life in Charlottesville was like living in a carefully constructed bubble, where the exigencies of the outside world were exiled for nine months of the year. Thus, as of 1966, UVA was still far removed from the turmoil that was enveloping most college campuses across the United States due to the burgeoning civil rights and anti-Vietnam War movements.

Yet in less than four years, most everything would change. In some sense, what occurred in Charlottesville was a microcosm of what was happening throughout our country, but at UVA the trajectory of change was greater in that it had started years later than in most places.

*left: Mr. Jefferson's Academical Village circa 1966*

1

I like to say that in these few years, a university characterized by the three "B's"—Blazers, Big Weekends and Bourbon—became a school respectively characterized by the three "D's"—Denim, Demonstrations and Drugs. And reflective of the current climate in our nation, more so than in any intervening period, social and political agendas began to take precedence over collegiality and civility.

Accordingly, I believe it is fair to say that my four years as an undergraduate at UVA were the most transformative and tumultuous four-year period in the history of the University. I witnessed the demise of a lifestyle that had existed for scores of years and the birth of a new one, which would evolve into the University we see today. The Old U was dead, and the modern UVA was born. And like any major life-cycle change, the event was full of disruption and turmoil.

Moreover, it was during this period that the seeds of incivility and rancor were sown that have blossomed so fully in our current environment.

This book is the story of those four years. It is part memoir and part history, both anecdotal and didactic, with a dash of gratuitous commentary. While it is a story told through my eyes, I like to think that I am in a uniquely strong position to tell it. First, my memories of that period are still extraordinarily vivid. Perhaps this is because everything I encountered at UVA was so new and different to me. In truth, this story has been percolating inside me for decades. Second, since I arrived at the University as a total outsider with no preconceived notions, I feel I was pretty much an objective observer of the events transpiring around me. In addition, I was broadly involved in most aspects of student life at the University, and as a journalist and student leader was personally involved in many, if not most, of the events I write about here. And finally, as one who truly never left the University in heart or spirit, and one who has remained closely involved with UVA over the past four decades, I believe I can also provide a measured view of how this period fits in with the course of the University's history.

My hope is that this book will transport the reader back to that time period and give one a sense of what it was really like to live through what is arguably the most extraordinary period in the University's history, a period that speaks profoundly to today's world. In so doing, I will hereby issue a "trigger warning"—as UVA's culture in 1966 was about as politically incorrect as it gets, and I don't intend to pull any punches. So with that in mind, please join me as we enter the literary time machine and set the controls for: Time: 1966; Place: Charlottesville, Virginia.

# PROLOGUE

I am often asked how a nice Jewish boy from a public high school in Fresh Meadows, Queens, found his way down to UVA—that well-known bastion of Southern gentility. It is actually a very good question. Nobody from my family had ever attended Virginia. Nobody from my high school had ever gone to UVA. I did not know one person who was at UVA or had ever been a student there. I had never set foot on the Grounds[1] until I arrived for first year orientation, although I had visited Monticello as a child on a family road trip. In fact, one probably could not find two more dissonant communities in the U.S. in 1966 than Queens, New York, and Charlottesville, Virginia. In trying to answer this question, I have finally concluded that it was a perfect storm of a half dozen or so factors.

First was the fact that my high school allowed each student to apply to only three schools plus a New York City public college. Particularly from the viewpoint of today's world, this seems incomprehensible. Can you imagine trying to explain to parents in Alexandria, Scarsdale or Greenwich that their daughter or son can only apply to three colleges? At best you would have a flood of equal protection lawsuits—more likely you would have the school board tarred and feathered. But back in Queens in 1966, most parents were first-generation Americans or immigrants themselves and were just happy to see their children go to

---

1   The University of Virginia has its own particular vernacular. The campus at UVA is always referred to as the "Grounds," the term "campus" never to be uttered in connection with Thomas Jefferson's creation. Likewise, UVA students are referred to as "first-year," "second-year," etc. rather than as "freshmen," "sophomores," etc. And our founder is referred to as "Mr. Jefferson," as if he still perambulates around the Grounds on a regular basis. Indeed, the heart of Thomas Jefferson still beats strongly in Charlottesville.

college. They wouldn't think of raising a stink.

Now, with all due modesty, I had a very impressive high school record. This was particularly the case back in 1966, before applying to college was like being vetted for a presidential cabinet position or becoming an astronaut. Academically, I was in the top three percent of my class of 700 and had strong college boards. As a journalist, I had won awards from the New York Times and Overseas Press Club. I also had a varsity letter. Thus, I reasonably believed that I had a good shot at being admitted to a top-tier school.

So how to choose the three schools to apply to? It is important to remember that applying to colleges in the sixties was not the same circus it is in modern times. The now popular Phileas Fogg-like journey to visit a dozen or more college campuses was not in vogue then. Indeed, my family made not one college campus jaunt—which was not unusual. I knew no one who went off on multiple college fact-finding expeditions. In fact, except for one unusual circumstance, I had not visited another college prior to my setting foot in Charlottesville. I obtained all knowledge of the college universe from the brochures I had sent away for, from a few commercial college guides and from advice from my older brother Steve, who had just graduated from Indiana University and who strongly advised me to escape from the NYC "ghetto." Our high school college guidance counselor added no value, his expertise not extending beyond a fifty-mile radius of New York City. Notwithstanding this limited pool of information, my top two choices were relatively easy.

The dream of most young Jewish boys in New York City was to go to an Ivy League school—sort of from Kiev to Columbia in one generation. However, I knew enough to realize that the top tier of the Ivy's was out of reach. Francis Lewis High School had never sent a student to Harvard, Princeton, or Yale in its five years of existence. Thus, my focus was on the Ivy second tier—and a number of occurrences made the choices clear. At that time, Cornell sponsored a recruiting event called Cornell Day, whereby one rising senior from each high school in

New York was chosen to spend a weekend in Ithaca. I won the competition in my school and spent a weekend at Cornell, where I saw country blues singer Josh White in concert, stayed at the Zeta Psi fraternity house and generally had a great time. Subsequently, I received a letter from Cornell requesting that I submit an application. While the letter noted that admission could not be assured, it also noted that most Cornell Day attendees were in fact admitted. Thus, I felt that I had a fairly strong lock on Cornell.

My reach school would be Dartmouth. As was the case with Cornell, I had been chosen by my school to represent it at a Dartmouth Day function. This was not as elaborate as the event staged by Cornell—it was a one-day event held at the Dartmouth Club in Manhattan. Nevertheless, I felt it gave me a leg-up at Dartmouth and a decent shot at admission. So with Cornell and Dartmouth as my first two choices, I had to find an attractive "safety" school.

The broad criteria for my third choice was a quality school a step below the Ivies, with a strong liberal arts program (especially in history and government, my likely majors), and located within a day's drive of NYC. Most of the schools that fit that bill were small men's liberal arts schools located in the Northeast, like Bowdoin, Bates, Hamilton, Colgate, and Bucknell. Looking southward, at the outer edge of the geographical radius, were Washington and Lee and UVA. Today one would certainly question considering Virginia as a safety school, particularly as an out-of-state resident. But in 1966, admission to UVA was not as selective as it is presently. While that was probably true for most top-tier schools nationwide, as college selectivity has dramatically increased over the past few decades, it was particularly true of UVA. Today, admission to UVA as an out-of-state student is as difficult, or perhaps even more difficult, as it is to most Ivies. But that was not the case in 1966. There are several reasons for that, one being that Virginia took a higher proportion of out-of-staters back then—about forty-five percent of the class compared to about thirty percent today. In any event, rightly or wrongly, I viewed UVA as a suitable safety school.

Why did I finally pick UVA as my third choice? In retrospect, I believe there were two main factors. First, as I was a budding libertarian, Thomas Jefferson was one of my heroes. I remember visiting Monticello as a child and buying a wall hanging of Mr. Jefferson's "sayings." It immediately went up in my bedroom and hung there until my parents moved out of my childhood home in 1998. My favorite Jefferson saying was, "The government that governs best, governs least."[2] Thus, actually attending Thomas Jefferson's University was quite attractive to me. But, perhaps a more compelling reason was that UVA seemed so different—so very Southern and traditional. Now, this would have been a turn-off for most of my contemporaries in Queens, where people tended to be very New York provincial—I mean the type of folks who would pack toilet paper for a trip to St. Louis or Atlanta. However, I had actually enjoyed my family's numerous trips to the historic sites in Virginia and to visit my aunt in small town Georgia. In fact, I found the prospect of going to school in an entirely different atmosphere somewhat exhilarating and, in many ways, I would welcome rather than regret leaving the New York cocoon. UVA certainly fit the bill as a potential major lifestyle change. But, truthfully, at the point when I chose Virginia as my safety school, I did not really believe it would come to that. I figured that Cornell was pretty much in the bag—end of story. What I hadn't taken into account in my naïveté, however, was another factor—which in reality would be the deciding one that set me on the road to Charlottesville.

The fact of the matter was that the Ivies still had Jewish quotas in the 1960s. It wasn't formal or written in stone and it was different at each school, but it existed. The quotas were particularly onerous for Jewish students from public schools in NYC, where the number of qualified applicants may well have resembled a tidal wave about to crash against their ivory towers. But I was ignorant of this at the time, and as the spring arrived in my senior year, I eagerly looked for-

---

2   While that quote was on the wall hanging, and is often attributed to Mr. Jefferson, my subsequent understanding is that it has never actually been found in any of his writings.

ward to receiving my response letters from Ithaca and Hanover. The Dartmouth rejection came first, which did not totally surprise me as I knew that my application was somewhat of a push. But when that was quickly followed by a rejection from Cornell, I was flabbergasted. Hadn't they sent me a letter requesting that I apply? I can still remember my anger and frustration and my reflections on the questionable ancestry of the admissions officer. However, my disappointment was somewhat assuaged shortly thereafter with the arrival of my acceptance to UVA. With the full exuberance of youth, it did not take long for me to forget the thumbs down from the Ivies and to fully embrace the prospect of becoming a Virginia Cavalier. In fact, as the weeks passed and I began to read more about UVA, my excitement increased measurably. Part of it was just the anticipation of going away to college, but part was also the mystery of knowing that I was about to enter a world totally distinct from anything I had encountered up to that point in my life.

~~~~~

During the summer, I received the notice of my dorm and roommate assignments. I can remember opening the letter and looking at the name of my prospective roomie—Bronson Percival—and not knowing which was his given and which his surname. Had they put his given name first or last? So was it Bronson Percival or Percival Bronson? You see, where I came from, folks didn't have two surnames. Their names were Tom O'Reilly or Frank DeSantis or Paul Goldberg. This was like a name out of the Scarlet Pimpernel. As I put the letter down and looked at my fellow counselors at the camp where I was working, all of whom were city kids, a big smile swept across my face as I realized I would shortly be heading in a major new direction.

# —FIRST YEAR—
## THE OLD U
### *1966-1967*

## The Journey Begins

My preparation for going away to college in 1966 bears little resemblance to the planning and machinations that accompany this experience in today's world. The logistics involved in an initial college move these days appear only a little less complicated than General Eisenhower's planning for Operation Overlord. Back then, it was really quite simple. Technology had not yet come to the forefront of everyday life. There were no such things as personal computers (much less laptops) or cell phones or microwaves. You were not allowed to have any electrical equipment in the first-year dorms other than a desk lamp, a radio, a phonograph (remember those?), a heating coil, a fan and, if you were affluent, an electric typewriter. No refrigerators, toasters, air conditioners or TVs allowed. The University provided linen service, so only a pillow and blanket were necessary.

The only preparatory work that I had to do was as a result of UVA being a "coat and tie" school (more on that later). I thus had to make some serious additions to my scanty wardrobe. Since I owned only one sport coat and had not bought a suit since my bar mitzvah four and a half years earlier, there was a bit of shopping to do. Fortunately, my older brother, Steve, who had some sense of collegiate fashion, was there to assist me. Thus, newly wardrobed, I packed my one suitcase, one suit bag, my blanket and pillow, my typewriter (manual), my new phonograph, a few record albums and I was ready to go.

First-year orientation began on Saturday September 10, 1966. Summer orientation and pre-registration were only figments of some administrator's imagination. Indeed, as we packed our family's 1964 Buick Skylark on September 8 for our journey down to Charlottesville,

I was filled with much anticipation, and I must admit some trepidation, to be setting foot for the first time on the Grounds of the University of Virginia. Thus began the first of what would be dozens of drives from NYC to Charlottesville. Since we left on a Thursday and my father could not take two days off from work, my brother volunteered to drive me down. I can basically do the drive now on auto-pilot—down the New Jersey Turnpike, across the Delaware Memorial Bridge (which at that time had only one span, causing horrific traffic jams during holidays), through Delaware and Maryland on Interstate 95, around D.C. on the beltway and finally into Virginia on a relatively newly opened Interstate 66. Route 66 took us to the home stretch—Route 29 South—which we picked up at the then-sparsely populated railroad crossroads of Gainesville. At that time, Route 29 was virtually all a two-lane road. Being our first trip to Charlottesville, we had not gauged our time appropriately and stopped for the night at the Howard Johnson's in downtown Warrenton.[3]

We arose early the next day and did the final hour and a half drive to Charlottesville. Today, looking at the commercial sprawl up Route 29 north of Charlottesville, it is difficult to imagine the emptiness and solitude of the journey. In 1966, Charlottesville's northern boundary was the recently constructed shopping center at Barracks Road. There was very little of anything between there and Culpeper 45 miles away. As we passed Barracks Road, we saw the newly opened University Hall indoor stadium, passed the old indoor stadium Memorial Gym on our left and exited 29 up the hill to McCormick Road. We passed the engineering school on our left (they were just breaking ground for the chemistry building) and the physics building on our right (Bavaro and Ruffner halls did not yet exist). And there they stood—just as in the photos I had seen—the ten red brick, first-year McCormick Road dormitories.

---

3    In 1966, no bypasses existed on Route 29 en route to Charlottesville, so you were required to travel through the downtown areas of "metropolises" such as Warrenton and Culpeper.

We parked our car directly in front of the dorm complex. At that time, there was no divide in the middle of McCormick Road and there was perpendicular parking right in front of the dorms, so quite a few autos could park there. As we watched a number of other cars being unloaded, my brother helped me carry my sparse belongings up to the second floor of Humphreys House. We put the bags down, he patted me on my shoulder, shook my hand and was off back to NYC. And so I was truly on my own in strange surroundings for the first time in my life.

## McCormick Road

As you may discern from the above, moving into UVA as a first-year in 1966 had little in common with the carnival-like atmosphere that surrounds this event in present times. I have been fortunate enough to have moved two children into McCormick Road in subsequent years and could only be bemused by the sharp contrasts with my own experience. There were no upperclassmen offering to help carry my belongings, no beaming students handing out refreshments, no invitations to sundry receptions for incoming students. In fact, my initial reaction to my new home was one of surprise and disappointment.

In 1966, the entire first-year class lived in the McCormick Road dorm complex—the last year that this would be the case. The complex consists of ten dormitories constructed in neo-Georgian style around a grassy courtyard known as the Quad. It is situated just west of the central Grounds and was constructed in the post-World War II era to accommodate the large influx of students returning from the war. The dorms were first available for occupation for the fall 1950 session— although the story is that not all the dorms were quite ready and that some students had to reside for a period in Memorial Gymnasium. Eight of the dorms are comprised of four groups of two conjoined buildings in the shape of an L. The remaining two dorms are one-offs that anchor the north end of the Quad. Each dorm is named after a distinguished deceased member of the University faculty or administration—Echols, Humphreys, Page, Emmet, Kent, Dabney, Metcalf, Lefevre, Bonnycastle and Hancock. These names resonate with the history of UVA.

Each dorm has three floors, with each floor separated into two corridors by a central stairway and a common bathroom. There is also a lower floor that is partially on ground level and which at that time had a central lounge with a TV and either offices and/or additional dorm rooms (most of which were for scholarship athletes).

My room assignment was 217 Humphreys. As I walked into the dorm for the first time (there were no locks on any of the main entry doors—that came with co-education), I was immediately struck by the cold institutional motif of the interior, which was in sharp contrast to the Georgian brick, ivy-covered exterior of the dorms. It was all cinderblock, linoleum and metal—no carpeting or wood to be found anywhere. As I walked up the stairs to the second floor, the thought struck me that the common areas of the dorm bore an eerie resemblance to the corridors of the public schools I had attended in NYC, which was unfortunate and disappointing. As I entered my corridor and then my room, there was no difference—linoleum floors, cinderblock walls, metal doors, metal desks, metal beds, metal chest of drawers. I was not to encounter such blatantly institutional decor again until I accepted Uncle Sam's invitation for basic training at Fort Dix. Moreover, even the restroom resembled my later barracks bathroom, with its open communal showers and rows of sinks side by side. One difference was that the toilets did have stalls with doors on them, unlike the rows of unenclosed toilets at Fort Dix.

Each corridor in the McCormick Road dorms has eleven rooms—ten double-occupancy rooms for first-year students and a single occupancy room in the middle of the floor for the dorm counselor (in later years renamed resident advisors). The dorm counselor was an upperclassman whose main jobs were to guide the young first-year men through the transition of living on their own in unfamiliar surroundings, and subsequently being an all-around big brother and font of UVA information.

I met my counselor shortly after setting my bags down. Bob Tuke was an archetypal 1966 vintage Wahoo[4] coat and tie fraternity man. (Bob would later run unsuccessfully for U.S. senator from Tennessee in 2008.) Bob welcomed me, gave me a few initial pointers, cocked an eye at my NYC accent (which would diminish over time as a self-preservation reaction) and moved on to welcome other arriving students.

I proceeded to unpack my meager belongings and await the arrival of my roommate, Bronson Percival or Percival Bronson (I was still unsure of his correct name). Unpacking did not take long, and, unlike present times, there was nothing to put together or set up. Decades later, I can remember moving my daughter into Page House and being astonished by the extent of the elaborate electronic and furniture systems being constructed before my very eyes. I had not visited Lowe's or brought my non-existent power tools with me—and thus immediately felt my inadequacy as a parent.

None of that existed in the primordial McCormick Road Dorms. No one erected intricate shelving, loft, or sound systems. Personal computers, printers, etc. were still dreams in the minds of their creators. In fact, the dorms were not in today's jargon "user friendly." Rather, the focus was more on what you couldn't have or do than on what you could have or do. Thus, the Room Accommodations Terms and Conditions circa 1966 set forth a long list of "prohibited possessions," including "air conditioners, ice boxes, refrigerators, television sets, exterior radio aerials, cooking and heating appliances, heavy electrical appliances..." In line with those guidelines, it was also explicitly stated that no cooking or even warming of food was permitted.

Another device absent from your dorm room was a telephone. I realize that to a student generation that has his or her smart phone attached to a part of their body at all times, it is virtually unimaginable that life could go on in the modern era without 24/7 availability of immediate contact with whomever you wish. But that was the plain

---

4  The official nickname of the University of Virginia is the Cavaliers. However, UVA students have also been known as Wahoos since the end of the late 19th century.

fact—no telephones permitted in the dorm rooms. The only phone available was an open pay phone at the end of the corridor. One phone for twenty people and no privacy. The counselor was allowed a phone in his room, and this could be used for emergencies.

The absence of TVs, phones and other electronic amusements led to profound differences in the lifestyles of first-year students today and those of my era. Without TVs, laptops, game boxes, etc., most of us actually spent a significant amount of time interacting face to face with other human beings. And without an iPhone readily available or the existence of email or texting, there was far less communication with parents and thus far less "helicopter parent" activity.

The other major area of restrictive rules in the dorms related to visitors of the opposite sex. The rule was rather simple and direct—no female visitors were allowed in the corridors any time, any day. No open-door policy or any other policy—women strictly verboten! Any female guest had to be entertained in the downstairs lounge. This rule applied to the dorm counselors as well. And this prohibition was not a rule in name only—it was strictly enforced. Violation of the restriction meant expulsion from the dorms—which for a first-year man meant expulsion from the University, since first-year students were required to live in the dorms. Consequences of this rule included: 1) There was often more "athletic" activity going on in Bonnycastle Dell (a recreational field adjacent to the dorms) at 2 a.m. than there was at 2 p.m.; and 2) the Charlottesville motel owners had more business from students on certain weekends than from tourists visiting Monticello.

And now for the good news—there was one major positive that made life in the dorms in 1966 somewhat more civilized than it has been for the past few decades: the existence of regular maid service. Our rooms were cleaned daily except on weekends. And, if you subscribed to the optional linen service, your bed would be made for you with fresh linen every week. Now that was a luxury worth more than any TV or refrigerator.

Not long after I had settled into my room, the door opened and in walked my roommate, Mr. Percival, first name Bronson. As roommates, a more disparate pair was hard to find—but not in the manner one would have thought. At first glance, my new roomie matched his moniker—umpteenth generation American, father in the foreign service, bespoke tweed coats, etc. However, this book could not be judged by its cover. I realized something was amiss when one of his first actions was to put up a map of Red China on the wall. Indeed, I had as my newfound colleague one of the few dyed-in-the-wool first-year anti-traditionalists. Actually, his Red China map was a nice balance to my poster of William F. Buckley Jr., on whose mayoralty campaign I had worked the previous year. And so began a true "odd couple" relationship: one New York City public school outsider who was chomping at the bit to put on his coat and tie, pledge a fraternity and immerse himself in the timeless Virginia culture; and one son of the well-bred Eastern establishment who wanted nothing to do with UVA traditions or the established order in Charlottesville. Interestingly, after an understandably rocky beginning, we actually developed a rather comfortable roommate relationship as the year progressed. Unfortunately, this friendship was to be short lived, as Bron, not surprisingly, transferred to Berkeley after our first year. An example of "if the shoe fits, wear it."

Having established an initial tenuous equilibrium in 217 Humphreys, I left my room and set out to meet the other members of the UVA first-year class.

## Introducing the Class of 1970

The first-year incoming undergraduate class in 1966 consisted of 1,258 students—917 in the College of Arts & Sciences (the "College"), 285 in the engineering school, and 56 in the School of Architecture. Thus, the class was about one-third the size of its current counterpart. While it is generally agreed that UVA in 1966 had not attained the academic standing it now holds (many of my classmates chuckle that they would never be admitted to UVA today), it was still considered a highly competitive school. The entering class was chosen from more than five thousand applicants and had an acceptance rate that was quite low for a state university. Average SAT scores in the College were 601 verbal and 638 math—very respectable in the era before College Board scores were "recentered."[5]

The defining characteristic of the class was that it was one hundred percent male. When people hear that today, they are inevitably amazed. How was it possible that a state university could be all male as late as 1966? In retrospect, it actually is fairly astounding. At that time, UVA was the only major state university that still had an exclusively male entering class. And, as it turned out, the class of 1970 would be the last to graduate in an all-male undergraduate community. As we shall see, UVA began admitting first-year undergraduate women in the fall of 1970.

While having a single-sex state university in 1966 was an anomaly, single-sex schools were still quite common among the top colleges in the United States. For example, six of the eight Ivy League colleges were all male. The University of Pennsylvania was in transition and only Cornell had a fully coeducational undergraduate school. Many, if not most, of the smaller liberal arts schools in the East and South were also all male—Amherst, Williams, Wesleyan, Bowdoin, Hamilton, Colgate, W&L and Davidson, to name just a few. In reality, UVA, with an undergraduate enrollment of about forty-five hundred in 1966, had more in common with these schools than with most other state universities. Nevertheless, and importantly, the lack of coeducation at UVA was more pronounced than at many of these other schools since we were more geographically isolated. Our sister school, Mary Washington in Fredericksburg, was over an hour and a half away by car, and the closest women's college, Mary Baldwin, was still a forty-mile trip over the Blue Ridge Mountains on two-lane roads. This was in marked contrast to many other all-male schools, which were either in big cities

---

5　In 1995, the College Board scores were modified or "recentered" to "reflect the contemporary test-taking population" (or, in common language, to make the Gen X students feel better about themselves). For example, a pre-recentered verbal score of 600 was translated into a score of 670.

or were within a few miles of women's or coed schools (i.e., Harvard, Yale, Brown, Columbia, Amherst). The profoundly all-male character of UVA would color virtually every aspect of life on Grounds.[6]

The second major characteristic of our class concerned its diversity—or rather the lack thereof. Actually, the concept of "diversity" as currently understood did not exist as a discussion point in 1966. To the extent that diversity was mentioned, it was in terms of geographical and not racial or ethnic diversity. Applying current definitions of diversity to the Class of 1970 would find that it was basically non-existent. As one of my classmates recently said to me, "Diversity at UVA when we arrived consisted of white Anglo-Saxon non-Episcopalians." Perhaps an exaggeration—but not by much. Racial and ethnic class statistics were not published back then, but I did my own analysis by delving into the Gardner Archives (I maintain an extensive collection of period ephemera) and retrieving my first-year facebook, which contained the photos, names, dorms, and hometowns of the members of the entering class. Over ninety percent of my class had their photos in the book—the names without photos listed at the end numbered only 120. Upon reviewing row after row of well-barbered visages bedecked in coat and tie, I could find only six black students, four Asian students and perhaps two students of Hispanic heritage. While there might have been a few more black students in the 120 names without photos, I believe it is safe to say that there were fewer than ten black students in the class[7] and that the total "minority" population barely exceeded one percent.

Looking back, it is particularly distressing to imagine a state with a black population approximating twenty percent having less than one

---

6  There actually were a few undergraduate women at the University in the nursing and education schools. However, since both those schools required two years of prior undergraduate study, the only women were those who transferred in from other schools for their third year of studies. There was one women's dorm—Mary Munford Hall (now part of the International Residential College).

7  Former Dean of Admissions Ernie Ern, who began his tenure in 1967, has noted that the 1967 entering class had only six black students out of eight that had received admissions from a total of twelve black applicants.

percent black representation at its premier state university. However, in context, it was not surprising. The Old Dominion was just emerging from the days of "massive resistance" to school integration. The first black undergraduate at UVA did not enroll until the mid-1950s after the Brown v. Board of Education Supreme Court decision, and the first black student in the College did not enroll until 1962. Virginia's then-current political culture was well illustrated by the fact that the Commonwealth's two Democratic senators, Byrd and Robertson, both voted against the landmark 1964 Civil Rights Act. While I remember being somewhat surprised by the virtual non-existence of black students at UVA, this in fact did not represent a deviation from my prior experience in supposedly liberal NYC. I did a similar "facebook" analysis of my high school graduation yearbook and found that, out of a graduating class of approximately seven hundred students, there was a total of three blacks, five Asians, and, as far as I could tell, no Hispanics. The great difference when compared to my new UVA class was that in my high school virtually all my classmates were "ethnic" whites—Irish and Italian Catholics and Eastern European Jews—rather than the "WASPs" that represented the great bulk of the students at Virginia.

In retrospect, applying more current views of diversity, it is reasonable to say that I was "diversity" at UVA in 1966. As a Jewish kid from a public high school in NYC, I was about as far from the norm as was evident on Grounds. This concept was brought home to me shortly after arriving at UVA, when one of my classmates would often greet me with "How are you doing, Joel, you ol' Jew?" While I believe this was not said with an intent to demean me, it was a salutation I did not hear often in Queens.

Well, I was no longer in my neighborhood "ghetto" in a situation where being Jewish meant being in the majority, but rather in a student population where less than ten percent were of the Hebraic faith, where Sunday morning brunch was no longer bagels and lox but rather a slab of Smithfield ham on a bed of grits, and where a typical celebratory greeting was no longer "mazel tov" but rather "congratulations, y'all."

To paraphrase Judy Garland in another classic film: "Toto, I've a feeling we're not in the Big Apple anymore." And, as we shall see, this reality would become more starkly evident when fraternity rush started.

However, there was one area that was arguably more diverse in the sixties: geographic diversity. In 1966, forty-five percent of the incoming undergraduate class were out-of-state students. This fact reflected a determined policy in favor of geographic diversity that harkened back to the Jeffersonian concept of UVA being a national institution. However, within a few years, with the advent of coeducation and the ever-increasing academic standing of the institution, pressure mounted from the state legislature to significantly increase the percentage of in-state students. Accordingly, the percentage of out-of-staters soon dropped to forty percent, then to thirty-five percent and now to a number below thirty percent. Thus, while the racial and ethnic diversity of UVA has materially increased in the past fifty years, Mr. Jefferson's wish for UVA to be a truly national institution has floundered.

In any event, for me personally, my new classmates represented a much more diverse group of people than I had known previously. Students from small towns in Mississippi, Kentucky, and Virginia, prep-schoolers from Choate, Deerfield, and Woodberry, serious scholarship football and basketball players—this was all so different from the universe of people I had been exposed to in Queens. It was exactly what I had been looking for—and like Dorothy in Oz, each moment brought a totally new experience.

## *Orientation*

Orientation Week began with move-in day on Saturday, September 10 and continued through Wednesday, September 14, encompassing first-year counseling, registration, Convocation, and lectures on customs and traditions and the Honor System. Since neither summer orientation or pre-registration existed back then, Orientation Week involved quite a bit of both getting acquainted with one's surroundings and administrative machinations. In the context of today's academic schedule, it is initially interesting to note that classes did not start until mid-September—almost three weeks later than they do presently. So one might think that the school year was shorter back then. In actuality, the academic year in the late sixties was a number of weeks longer than it is now. The lost time at the beginning of the academic year was more than made up by a much-shorter winter break, no October reading-days break, and the academic year ending weeks later than it does at present. So, as we shall see below, today's families are paying significantly more comparable tuition for less time in the classroom.

Course registration took place in Memorial Gym, where long lines of students waited to choose and then submit individual hole-punched computer cards for each chosen course. Course decisions for first-years were relatively limited due to the high number of required courses and the fact that advanced placement credits (which were still in their relative infancy) were not yet widely utilized. Today it is common for students to place out of many, if not most, of their required courses. In 1966 it was relatively rare for students to place out of any of their requirements,[8] which included writing composition, two semesters of literature (American and English), two semesters of a lab science, two semesters of math, two semesters of history and foreign language proficiency.

Another reason why course decisions were simpler was that there were far fewer courses to choose from. A comparison of course offerings in the College in the late 1960s with those available currently show an enormous disparity that goes well beyond the growth in the student population. Both the number of faculty and number and diversity of courses have grown exponentially over the decades. For example, the Department of Religion had two faculty members and offered about fifteen different courses in 1966—the comparable numbers for the Department of Religious Studies today are about thirty-five faculty members and over a hundred courses. Similarly the art department

---

8  The exceptions were the esteemed few chosen as Echols Scholars, who were relieved of most of their required courses.

had four faculty members and offered eighteen courses compared to thirty-six faculty and about sixty course offerings now.

In regard to devising one's schedule, I am aware through my children's experiences at the University that in recent years an important factor has been the avoidance of Monday and Friday classes. Not only was that not a widespread practice back then, but in fact Saturday classes were still routinely being held. My biology lectures were held at 9 a.m. on Tuesdays, Thursdays and Saturdays. The Saturday morning lectures generally witnessed a significant reduction in attendance—particularly on party weekends. In full knowledge of this practice, Mr. Hamilton[9] would inevitably base a disproportionate number of his test questions on lectures held the Saturday mornings of party weekends.

In addition to the course requirements mentioned above, students were required to take two non-credit semesters of physical education. The phys ed department offered such courses as touch football, softball, bowling, beginning swimming (for those unable to complete the seventy-yard swimming test), soccer, etc. Phys ed was viewed as a serious requirement. Even varsity athletes were exempt from only one of the two-semester requirement. For some reason, the phys ed requirement became a target for attack by the progressive/radical movement a few years later and was shortly thereafter phased out. To this day, I really don't understand why this was part of the progressive agenda. I never figured going bowling or playing soccer to be a liberal versus conservative issue. Frankly, while some first-years complained about phys ed cutting into their sleeping or nap times, it was probably the only source of physical activity for many, other than dancing or bending their elbows. Indeed, the phys ed requirement was merely following Mr. Jefferson's invocation, "A strong body makes the mind strong."

Part of the registration process was paying for tuition and room rent. Incredible as it may seem now, my tuition and fees for the College

---

9  Members of the faculty were addressed as "Mister" rather than "Professor." I would add, it could have been "Mrs." or "Miss" (the term "Ms." had not yet entered common parlance), but truthfully in my four years of undergraduate study at UVA, I never had a course with a female instructor.

of A&S as an out-of-state student was $1,037 for the entire year. For in-state students it was $452. The corresponding rates for 2016-17 are $45,066 for out-of-staters and $15,722 for Virginians. This represents an astonishing increase in tuition costs for families, well outstripping inflation. The general inflation rate from 1966 to the present is about 650%. Applying that rate to the 1966 numbers, out-of-state and in-state tuition and fees would be about $7,500 and $3,400 respectively. What a world of difference from the $45,000+ and $15,000+ being forked over today. The causes for this extraordinary disparity are legion, and the subject for a separate book. But, it can be noted that a large measure of the increase in tuition is due to a corresponding decrease in state funding for the University. In the past thirty years, state funding for UVA has decreased from about twenty-eight percent to about six percent of the operating budget. Add to that the costs of accelerating technologies, the tremendous increase in course offerings and the growth of administrative bureaucracies and you have some idea of the "whys."

~~~~~

Three group meetings during orientation involved the entire incoming class. The first was Convocation, which was held at the recently completed University Hall ("U Hall"). So for the initial gathering of the Class of 1970, all thousand-plus of us donned our coats and ties and headed to U Hall.

## Coats and Ties

In late August 2016, as I was driving over to Barracks Road, I stumbled on the entering class of 2020 marching down Alderman Road past the now-superseded University Hall toward their own class orientation meeting at JPJ (John Paul Jones Arena). The contrast between this group and my group almost fifty years earlier couldn't have been more striking. More females than males, a broad spectrum of races and ethnicities, and virtually every one of them clad in shorts and T-shirts.

Interestingly, I believe that of all these stark contrasts, the one that would have shocked us most if we had been able to look into the future would have been the attire, or lack thereof, worn by the entering first-years.

The coat-and-tie tradition was one of the pillars of the Old U. Stretching back for generations, Virginia Gentlemen wore coats and ties to classes, meetings, and functions around the Grounds. Significantly, this was a tradition, not a rule like at Yale, where in 1966 Yalies were still required to wear a coat and tie to dinner. And because it was a tradition rather than a regulation, you did not have those opposing the rule mocking it as they did at Yale, by wearing a coat and tie with a T-shirt or sweatshirt. If one did not want to wear a coat and tie on Grounds, that was his choice. But in 1966, most men at UVA bought into the Virginia Gentleman ethos and the traditions that embodied it. These key traditions were best captured by a paragraph in *The Jeffersonian*, a soft cover manual published by the UVA YMCA and handed out at orientation:

> The three most important traditions prevailing in University life today are: 1. a deep and abiding respect for the individual and an insistence that the individual accept responsibility for his decisions and actions, 2. an unmistakable emphasis and insistence upon the individual accepting the honor system as a way of life, 3. an emphasis on good taste and good manners.

The coat-and-tie tradition was a reflection of the third leg of this tradition trinity. Dressing up for classes and functions was a statement that one respected the institution, the art of learning, and each other. As *The Jeffersonian* further stated, "The [coat and tie] tradition is not based on a slavish love for an outmoded past, but is rooted in the belief that to dress neatly and acceptably for any occasion is a sign of individual maturity, self discipline, and good taste."

Few, if any, in 1966 could imagine that the upheavals that would take place within a few short years would so totally eviscerate this tradition that by 1970 it was virtually gone. Some hard-core Old U types still wore coats and ties my last year, but adherence to this generations-old practice probably dropped from around ninety-five percent in 1966 to around twenty-five percent by 1970. Some might call this "progress," but if progress is measured by the substitution of the self-discipline, neatness, and mutual respect reflected in the wearing of coats and ties with the comfort, ease, and general grunge reflected in the wearing of shorts, T-shirts and ripped jeans, then future historians will have an interesting time in defining "progress" in this regard.

But back to 1966 and the sartorial splendor on display daily on the Grounds. Not surprisingly, as in most defined subcultures, certain types of acceptable attire were favored over others. Before arriving at UVA, my brother had found an article for me in *Men's Wear* magazine (a copy of which resides in the Gardner Archives) in which students from a few selected colleges wrote a letter to an imaginary incoming student telling him what should constitute his wardrobe. Virginia was one of the schools represented and the "letter," written by third-year man Alfred Berkeley[10], is a snapshot in time of the prevailing wardrobe of your typical Wahoo. Berkeley provided great detail as to each category of apparel for a well-dressed UVA student, which included the following:

Suits: "For winter, bring one dark three-piece suit. It must have three buttons, natural shoulders and a center vent. For spring, the style and color are the same, just drop the vest and look for a lighter weight."

Sport coats: "Two sport coats for winter and two for spring should meet your needs. Pick a wool tweed herringbone and either a blue blazer or Shetland plaid for winter. For spring, a poplar blazer, seersucker or madras."

---

10   Al Berkeley would later become President of the NASDAQ Stock Exchange. He also participated in one of the most infamous pranks in UVA history. In 1965, a cow mysteriously appeared on the roof of the Rotunda. The perpetrators were not identified at the time. Over thirty years later, Berkeley admitted that he and some of his fraternity brothers were responsible.

Slacks: "For each sport coat, get two pairs of dark dressy slacks. Then get four pairs of khakis for class. At Virginia, pants have vertical pockets that are part of the seam, belt loops, cuffs and a 17-inch taper. Forget about Continental, forget about Western."

Shirts: "Since you'll be wearing coats and ties so frequently, make sure you have at least ten long-point button-down shirts. You'll find more use for solids, so about six of your shirts should be white then maybe some blues, a maize and some stripes or tattersall checks."

Ties: "Choose about ten ties and include printed paisley challis and foulards, striped reps and club ties."

Shoes: "The shoes that will get you through every situation are a pair of plain or wing-tipped shell cordovans, a pair of penny loafers or tassle cordovan slip-ons, a pair of tennis shoes and a pair of boots for snow."

The article also contained suggestions for outer coats, raincoats, dress coats, umbrellas and even what was appropriate underwear: "Your underwear won't make or break you as a B.M.O.C. [big man on campus], but it's not a bad idea to buy T-shirts rather than old men's 'basketball jersey' undershirts ... and boxer shorts, not 'little boy' briefs."

So now you have a good idea as to the appearance of your typical UVA student in 1966. Of course, not everyone conformed to (or could afford) Mr. Berkeley's suggestions, but there is no doubt that most UVA Gentlemen could be found traversing the Grounds in their blazers or plaid sport jackets, white, blue or pink button-down shirts adorned with a rep or club tie, khaki pants and ever present Weejuns penny loafers. While one might argue that this was all very conformist, it is at least this author's opinion that there was more variety in the coat-and-tie era than in the succeeding jeans and work shirt or shorts and T-shirt eras. In any event, it certainly took more time in the morning to choose one's outfit.

~~~~~

Following the Convocation ceremonies at U Hall, we exited the arena and were greeted by an astounding sight. On the hillside in the distance was a large burning object in the shape of the letter Z. I had no idea what this meant—although I knew I was in the South and there was a regional history of burning symbols in the night. So I turned to one of my new classmates and asked him if he knew what that was. Looking down at me as if I was some type of foreigner (which I guess I was) he said, "Don't you know, that's the mystical Z, the symbol of one of the U's secret societies. Those are the top men on Grounds— you needn't be much concerned with that, Yankee." So that was my introduction to the existence of the various indigenous honoraries and societies, secret and not so secret, that existed at UVA.

*The flaming Z*

## *Rings, Ribbons, and Sevens*

I quickly learned that there was a certain social hierarchy at UVA that had existed for decades. The fraternity system set the broad frame-work for this hierarchy (more of that later). But sitting above the fra-ternities were a group of honoraries and societies that defined what a B.M.O.C. was on Grounds. A number of schools have such groups— Skull and Bones at Yale, the Order of the Golden Fleece at Chapel

Hill, Michigamua at the University of Michigan—but I am not aware of any school that has as many groups with such a fabled history as existed at UVA in 1966 and as exist still. The most renowned of these groups were the two "ring" societies (Z and IMP), the two "ribbon" societies (Eli Banana and T.I.L.K.A.) and the Seven Society—the only true secret society of the lot back then. The orientation issue of *The Cavalier Daily*, the UVA student newspaper (commonly referred to as the *CD*), had this to say about these groups: "Membership in one of these societies is one of the highest honors that a student can achieve while at the University."

The two ribbon societies[11] are the oldest honoraries on Grounds. The Eli Banana Society was founded in 1878 and T.I.L.K.A. in 1889. The two are mutually exclusive, and historically there was heated competition between them for those perceived to be the top men at the University. Both groups tapped twice a year at that time—on the Thursday evening before Openings and Easters, two of the major party weekends (more on the "big weekend" syndrome later). The tapping ceremonies for both societies were quite entertaining and raucous: the Elis marching in their colorful robes with their leader, the "Grand Banana," banging on the Eli drum; and the T.I.L.K.A.s singing their traditional drinking song with their leader, the "Guru," holding aloft the original silver T.I.L.K.A. loving cup filled with beer. Both would march around the Grounds tapping each new member at his fraternity house or other designated location. If there was a difference between the two groups, it was that the T.I.L.K.A.s tended to give more weight to student leadership while the Elis looked more kindly on social and hell-raising skills.

Today's students no doubt would be surprised at the high profile the ribbon societies had at the Old U. An example of this was that the annual touch football game between the two societies, held in Mad Bowl on the Sunday afternoon after Openings Weekend, was front-

---

11  These groups were known as ribbon societies since their members originally wore colored ribbons on their sports or suit jackets—blue for the Elis and red for the T.I.L.K.A.s.

page news in the *CD*. In recent years, the Elis and T.I.L.K.A.s have become more social clubs than honoraries and are the domain of a few select fraternities. And, unlike the other honoraries noted, they remain all-male organizations. At least as far as the Elis are concerned, it is possibly due to the reality that if women were subjected to the traditional Eli initiation ceremony, it is more likely than not that various disciplinary actions would ensue. Notwithstanding this evolution, both societies remain committed to the University and its unique traditions and both have made substantial gifts to UVA in recent years.

*Hey! Hey! Hey!*
*T-I-L-K-A*

*The Elis marching*

The next step in the hierarchy of the honoraries are the ring societies—the Zs and IMPs. These organizations are much smaller than the ribbons, with each group choosing only about a half-dozen students a year for membership. Because the symbols of the two societies are omnipresent on the Grounds—painted on buildings, steps, fraternity houses—they are better known to the community at large than the ribbons. They are also more in the public eye because of their consistent philanthropy to the University, which has only increased with the passage of time. The elder of the two organizations, the Z Society, was founded in the late 19$^{th}$ century. Originally a ribbon society, it is said that it was formed to take the best members of the Elis and T.I.L.K.A.s. Its members shortly thereafter gave up wearing a ribbon for wearing a ring with the society's insignia. The group has been very secretive in its actions, with its members known only by the ring they wore and a list of its membership published each year in the University yearbook, the *Corks and Curls*. (More recently the Society became even more secretive with its members only wearing the ring and disclosing their identities upon graduation.) Members of the society have historically been leaders in student government, publications and athletics. The organization is well known for its philanthropy, for hosting numerous recognition dinners for students and faculty, and for granting various awards.

The IMP Society was founded in 1913 as a successor to the Hot Feet, a rowdy group that was expelled from the University in 1912. The IMPs have always been a more public and boisterous group than the Zs and are well known for parading around Grounds with their pitchforks and devil's horns, particularly during their annual coronation of the King IMP. While promoting "revelry" and initiating "pranks" are some of the stated objectives of the group, the IMPs have traditionally taken well-known student leaders as members and also host honorary dinners and dispense University-wide awards.

*Coronation of King IMP Pete Gray*

The only true "secret" society in the groups discussed above is the Seven Society. Members are only disclosed at the time of their death, which is then publicly noted by the University Chapel's bell tolling in increments of seven for seven minutes. Like the ring societies, the Seven's symbol appears in multiple locations around the University and, while a "secret" society, the organization has attained notoriety over the years through its philanthropy—often making very public monetary gifts in a dramatic fashion. These gifts usually have the number seven in them multiple times and often are placed in a location where the number seven comes into play—for example, below the seventh seat from the right in the seventh row of a seating plan. Unlike the ring and ribbon societies, the Sevens are not strictly a student organization, with members having been chosen also from the administration and faculty.

~~~~~~

After Convocation at U Hall, there remained one more group gathering before classes began. That was the address on the Honor System to be given by Dean T. Braxton Woody at Old Cabell Hall.

## *There Is No Degree of Honor*

The Honor System at Virginia in 1966 was the "Holy of Holies," often referred to as the University's "greatest treasure" and its "most cherished tradition." It was the central pillar of the Old U and the key element of what made UVA "UVA." I think it is difficult for those at the University today to understand the central role the Honor System played in the fabric of the institution and the passion it engendered. Thus, to understand the University of Virginia in 1966 and to comprehend the Old U, one must appreciate the place of the Honor System in the culture and how it functioned at the time. It was the ultimate expression of student self-government and being a Virginia Gentleman. In effect, it could be said that much of the ethos of UVA flowed from the group acceptance of the Honor Code.

Much has been written of the history of UVA's Honor System. How it emerged in the 1840s out of the chaos of student rowdiness and misbehavior, which culminated in the shooting of a professor on Mr. Jefferson's Lawn. How it evolved to be by the mid-twentieth century one of the most, if not the most, famous and respected college honor codes in the country. A contemporary issue of *Time* magazine had this to say in an article on cheating in everyday life: "[I]n a few schools and colleges there is practically no cheating at all. Perhaps the most famous of these is the University of Virginia.... Virginia is old fashioned enough for the old ideal of 'gentleman' to be given some meaning."

The Honor Code was more than just a set of rules and procedures. It was part of the soul of the institution. Famed alumnus Mortimer Caplin[12] put it like this in his honor address to the students in 1961:

---

12 Mortimer Caplin graduated in 1937 from UVA, where he was a member of Phi Beta Kappa and an intercollegiate boxing champion. He also graduated from the Law School, where he was Editor-in-Chief of the *Law Review*. He was a founder of the prestigious law firm of Caplin & Drysdale and served as IRS Commissioner under President Kennedy. He has served on the University Board of Visitors and has been a major donor to the University, particularly in the arts.

"We are talking about a way of life which is practiced here, which is ingrained in our daily existence, and which becomes a permanent part of us... never forgotten, wherever we go, whatever we do." And similarly, Bernard Mayo, professor of history and Jeffersonian scholar, asserted the following in his contemporary address entitled "Mr. Jefferson and the Way of Honor":

> The code of honor is much more than a few simple and obvious moral laws. Of far more significance—and this I cannot too strictly stress—is the spirit of the code. This is a positive, affirmative spirit. It is one of mutual trust and mutual respect which pervades every phase of University life and motivates men and women to conduct all their affairs on the high level of integrity, character and honor.

Both in terms of scope and procedure, the student-run Honor System was far different in 1966 than it is currently. This is not surprising, as the system has always been meant to reflect the beliefs and values of the current student body—and those beliefs and values, reflecting those of society at large, have witnessed a tidal wave of change. As far as scope, the code was relatively straightforward. While there was no written honor constitution (the first one was adopted in 1977), the substance of the system extant at the time was embodied in a document known as the "Blue Sheet," which was distributed to all incoming students (a copy of which resides in the Gardner Archives). The first paragraph of the Blue Sheet stated explicitly, "Lying, cheating or stealing or breaking one's word of honor under any circumstances are considered infringements of the Honor System." The operative phrase in the last sentence was "under any circumstances." There was no materiality concept as exists in the code today, where an honor violation is defined as a "Significant Act"—back then, stealing one dollar was treated the same as stealing a hundred dollars; cheating on one exam multiple-choice question was the same as cheating on them all. Once the transgression was considered to be within the purview of the system, any breach was considered to be significant. You were either an honorable person or not. Geographically, the code applied not only on Grounds, but to Charlottesville and anywhere else—be it New York, Chicago, London or Tokyo—where an individual represented himself or herself as a UVA student.

In order to avoid "overloading" the system, certain areas of behavior considered to be conduct unbecoming a gentleman were not considered to be within the scope of the code. Thus, the Blue Sheet noted that "many things reprehensible and heartily condemned by the Honor Committee and all good citizens" are not considered honor offenses. These included "drinking, sexual immorality, breaches of administrative regulations, failure to pay honest debts and breaches of civil contracts." Therefore, certain discreditable behavior was thought to be better handled by the University's Judiciary Committee (boorish or immoral behavior) or Bad Check Committee, or the civil or criminal courts (if violations of the law).

As one can see, there was in certain circumstances no clear demarcation between what was considered an honor offense and what was referred to other bodies for resolution. This difficult separation of jurisdictions was based on current student opinion, and the same exists to this day. Nevertheless, once on Grounds, it did not in fact take long to understand very well what behavior was verboten.

There were a number of other significant aspects of the Honor System that were materially different in 1966 than today. First was the mandate that any student who became aware of a possible honor violation had the absolute obligation to investigate and to accuse the offender to his or her face if evidence of guilt was found. This "non-toleration" feature of the system was one of the more controversial features of the code. Critics said the duty to investigate and accuse turned students into "snitches" and led to student "witch hunts." Notwithstanding these criticisms, the duty to investigate was integrally tied to the integrity of the system as being exclusively student run. And in 1966, it was totally and completely operated by students alone. Only a student could bring an honor charge against another student. If a faculty member believed a violation had occurred, he or she had to inform another student, who then had the obligation to investigate the matter. Such is no longer the case today—a faculty member may directly approach the Honor Committee with a potential violation. This is not surprising in view of the fact that the "non-toleration" aspect of the system is gone and students themselves are no longer obligated to investigate potential breaches of honor.

Another major difference was the strict adherence to the decades-old "single sanction" penalty. If a student admitted to having committed an honor violation or was found by the Honor Committee to have done so, there was only one remedy—immediate expulsion from the University. The single sanction has been criticized over the years, but in 1966 it was alive and well. Since that time, there has been a continuing dilution of the concept. First came the adoption of the concept of "conscientious retraction," whereby a student who has committed an honor violation but has not yet been accused can make amends and avoid expulsion. And then in 2013, a more significant deviation from the single sanction was approved by the student body—the "informed retraction." Pursuant to this change, a student charged with an offense can admit to the violation and take a two-semester leave of absence from the University. While the Honor Committee has called the informed retraction a "philosophical extension of the conscientious retraction," it is in reality much more than that. By allowing a student a lesser penalty after having been charged with a violation, this amendment really did end de facto the century-old mandate of the single sanction.

As regards procedure, the Honor System was enforced very differently then. Befitting the times, it was much simpler and to the point. Any student believing that a breach of the code had occurred had the obligation to investigate the matter. If after such investigation, it was believed there was no improper conduct, the matter was dropped and there were no further proceedings. On the other hand, if after such investigation, it was believed the suspect was guilty of a violation, the suspect was to be confronted and asked to explain his or her conduct. If after hearing the explanation, the investigator was still convinced of the suspect's guilt, he or she was required to demand the suspect student leave the University at once. The accused was then required to either leave or demand of the president of his or her school that the Honor Committee be convened to try the case.

The Honor Committee at that time consisted of the student presidents of the ten schools of the University. The chair of the Standing Committee was the President of the College of Arts & Sciences. When sitting upon a trial, the vice-president of the school of which the accused was a member constituted the eleventh member of the committee and the president of that school acted as the chair for that trial. The Honor Committee acted as both judge and jury for each trial. There was no right to a random student jury as exists today. If after a trial, nine of the eleven members of the committee reached a guilty verdict in a secret ballot, the accused was mandated to leave the University immediately. There were no appeals allowed—a case could be reopened only upon the production of new evidence bearing directly on the issue of guilt.

In any event, as I marched over to Old Cabell Hall in September 1966, I was not aware of past or future controversies regarding the intricacies of the Honor System. All I knew was what I had read in the pamphlet contained in my orientation material—that this was a century-old tradition, that it was taken very seriously and that I could be summarily punted from the University for a violation. I also did not anticipate that I was about to listen to one of the most profound and moving speeches I have ever heard.

We filed into Old Cabell Hall for the first time, all thousand-plus members of the Class of 1970, bedecked as usual in our coats and ties. Standing at center stage of the great auditorium dominated by the massive replica painting of Raphael's "School of Athens" was Dean T. Braxton Woody, his impeccably attired personage crowned with that great shock of pure white hair. In 1966, Dean Woody was approaching the end of a history with the University that dated back to 1919. He had graduated from UVA in 1923 and returned to begin his teaching career in 1928 as an assistant professor in the Department of Romance Languages. So when he mounted the podium in 1966, he had been associated with UVA for almost fifty years and had been teaching there for over thirty-five years. He was a beloved and extremely well-respected member of the University community, having just become the first recipient of the Alumni Association Distinguished Professor Award that very year.

*The Deans [L-R] - Irby Cauthen, Wayne Wallace, Ray Bice,*
*Braxton Woody, John Graham*

To this day, I am not quite sure why Dean Woody's talk had such a profound effect on me. Perhaps it was because it was an introduction to a way of life that I would find so satisfying and rewarding. And maybe it was because it struck an emotional chord that was waiting to be played. In fact, my parents had imbued me with the concept that "your word is your bond." For whatever reason, I can still remember sitting there transfixed by the sound of that cultured sonorous Southern accent (which was new to me at the time). Of course, I can't recall all the specifics of the speech, but I do remember some highlights. I recollect that toward the beginning of the speech Dean Woody talked about the non-toleration aspect of the code—the obligation to investigate and confront a suspected offender. No doubt this was highlighted up front since for most of us this was both a new and controversial concept. Dean Woody's comments were to the effect that it was not enough to follow the code oneself—it was each student's responsibility to uphold the "community of honor." I recall he strongly affirmed that doing this did not make one an "informer," since an informer is a person that "goes behind one's back." Here, you were obligated to confront the suspect directly to his or her face, a decidedly "difficult" and "courageous" act.

After that strong opening, the parts of the talk I remember most clearly were a story he told of a conversation with a distraught parent and then how he ended his speech. The story involved a mother who came to speak to him to plead for her son's future at the University, the student having unexpectedly returned home after being accused of an honor violation. The woman beseeched Dean Woody, saying that her son knew that he had made a mistake and wasn't it possible for him to have another chance. Dean Woody responded, "There are no second chances." But, the mother continued, "It was only a small error." To which Dean Woody replied (and I can remember this like I heard it yesterday), "Madam, you may think it was a small error, but, Madam"—and here he paused and stared straight out at the assembled crowd in a manner you knew meant something critical was coming. His hand slamming down on the podium to emphasize each word, he said, "THERE IS NO (slam) DEGREE (slam) OF HONOR (slam)!"

Well, you could have heard the proverbial pin drop. There you had it, the essence of the code. It was binary: either you are an honorable person or you are not. After that, everything else was somewhat anticlimactic except for Dean Woody's concluding invocation to uphold this "sacred treasure" that was passed down from generation to generation of UVA students. He told us that "we" sitting there were now the "custodians" of this "sacred trust," and he concluded with this injunction: "You must not, you cannot, you will not betray this trust."

As we filed out of Old Cabell Hall and looked out on the terraced majesty of Mr. Jefferson's Lawn, I could only wonder at this new and vastly different world I had thrust myself into. This world of gentlemen, coats and ties and honor codes was a different universe than the hardscrabble, rough-and-tumble world of New York City, where the equivalent of the Honor Code was "get away with what you can." It was a culture that I could reject, tolerate, or warmly embrace—and I think it was then and there, staring out at the Lawn and with Dean Woody's words still ringing in my ears, that I chose to embrace it. And, as it turned out, other than the influence of my parents, the UVA culture of honor would have the greatest impact on how I chose to live my life.

As for the Honor System at UVA, on the one hand, many would say that it has been in an ever-increasing downward spiral since the 1960s. Indeed, there is little doubt that Dean Woody's "sacred treasure" has been materially diluted in both content and application since that period. On the other hand, some would say that it is astonishing that the system still exists in any form given both the increase in size and diversity of the University and the overall societal diminution of traditional values that has occurred since the 1960s, which has only accelerated over the past decade. I think it is reasonable to judge the current state of the system as somewhere between those two points of view. While the strength and stature of the system has certainly eroded over the years, most current Wahoos still view the concept of honor as a pillar of their life at UVA and a defining attribute of the University.

And as for T. Braxton Woody, he gave his last honor address in 1968 and retired from teaching in 1971, but only after playing a significant role in UVA's decision to embrace co-education. We became friends during my fourth year, and I remember fondly the glasses of port and camaraderie we shared at each Raven Society[13] banquet through my

---

13 The Raven Society is yet another honorary indigenous to UVA. Founded in 1904, the society taps students, faculty and alumni based on scholarship, achievement and contributions to the University. The reference to the raven reflects Edgar Allan Poe's connection to UVA, where he was a student for one year, in 1826.

years at the Law School. I last saw him in 1995 after not having seen him for years. He was 94 years old at the time and looked great—in his ever-present coat and tie and still with that great shock of white hair crowning his head. Dean Woody passed away a few years later, in January 2000, and the Board of Visitors shortly thereafter wisely voted to name a new dormitory after him.

## The Lawn

*The timeless Lawn*

Dean Woody's honor address was the culmination of orientation week and classes began the following day. As a liberal arts student in the College, all but one of my classes were held in New Cabell Hall— the 1950s utilitarian complex built into the hillside behind Old Cabell Hall and, therefore, fortunately out of view from most vantage points on the Grounds. Thus, my daily walk to classes from McCormick Road took me onto the south end of the Lawn.

Even as a seventeen-year-old first-year student, I knew how lucky I was to be traversing one of the most beautiful and historic landscapes in the country.[14] For those reading this who have not visited UVA, the

---

14  Not surprisingly, Mr. Jefferson's Grounds were subsequently designated by UNESCO as the only collegiate World Heritage Site in the U.S.A. and only one of four in the world. The American Institute of Architects has called the Grounds "The proudest achievement of American architecture in the past 200 years."

Lawn is the epicenter of Mr. Jefferson's Academical Village. This multi-tiered rectangular plot is bordered on the east and west by Tuscan-style arcades connecting rows of individual dorm rooms interspersed by ten pavilions (five on each side), each constructed in a different neo-classical style. The pavilions (each an individual mansion in its own right) were originally used as classrooms and residences for professors and now are mostly homes for distinguished members of the faculty and administration. At the north head of the Lawn, at its highest elevation, stands the Rotunda, a neo-classical gem modeled after the Roman Pantheon and arguably Jefferson's crowning architectural achievement. The south end of the Lawn, which was originally left open to allow for magnificent panoramic views of the mountains, was unfortunately closed off at the end of the nineteenth century by the construction of Cabell, Rouss and Cocke halls after the infamous Rotunda fire of 1895.

The essence of this book is about change, but the Lawn is one thing at UVA that has been virtually timeless. Mr. Jefferson would hardly blink today if he were to stroll down the Colonnades toward the Rotunda. This patch of land is emblazoned in the heart and mind of every true Wahoo. I have walked the Lawn hundreds, if not thousands, of times in my seven years as a student, two stints as a UVA parent, forty-plus years as an alum and now as a part-time resident of Charlottesville. But each time I approach the Academical Village, walking down an alley bordered by Mr. Jefferson's famous serpentine walls, and emerge on the verdant splendor of the Lawn, I still find myself catching my breath as I try to digest the quiet magnificence of this amazing place. In a university that now has over twenty thousand students, there is still a serene, almost-bucolic quality to the Lawn—an escape from the "slings and arrows" of the outside world.

## *Don't Go Up to the Balcony*

One of the fellows on my corridor was a son of the football coach, and thus, living in town, occasionally had access to an auto.[15] Shortly after classes began, he invited me and a few others to go to a movie in downtown Charlottesville, about two miles away. This was pre-Downtown Mall Charlottesville, and there was no convenient public transport going between the Grounds and downtown. Thus, having a car was a necessity if downtown was your destination. So we piled into the treasured auto and headed to the Jefferson Theater, which was one of the two movie theaters downtown, along with the Paramount.[16]

At that time, downtown Charlottesville was already suffering the economic fallout from the opening of the Barracks Road Shopping Center just a few years earlier,[17] and I remember Main Street being nearly deserted.

After purchasing our tickets and going inside, a few of the fellows pulled out their ever-present packs of cigarettes.[18] Remembering that back home the smoking section was always in the balcony, I asked where the stairs to the balcony were. One of the guys said, "Don't go up to the balcony." I asked why not, and he just restated, "You don't go up there." We went into the main seating area and I noticed that, unlike at home, the smoking section was in the last four or five rows of the auditorium, which is where we sat. After the movie was over (no, I don't recall which film it was) and as we were leaving the theater, I noticed

---

15  In 1966 (as is the case today) first year students were prohibited from having automobiles.

16  Charlottesville, at that time, had only one additional theater—the University Theater—which was a small venue located at the east end of the Corner.

17  This phenomenon was happening all over small town America in the 1950s and 60s. The traditional main street shopping areas were being financially devastated by the newly constructed shopping malls with easier access and parking and a broader selection of goods and services in one place.

18  Statistics show that in the mid-1960s, over 40% of adults in the USA were smokers (that number now is around 15%). Many, if not most, of us at UVA were smokers at the time. Cigarettes were particularly cheap in Virginia in the 1960s—I remember them being a quarter a pack.

that everyone coming down from the separate balcony entrance was black. The fellow who told me not to go up to the balcony looked at me, cocked his head toward those folks, and smiled.

And that was my introduction to 1966 Charlottesville. What I witnessed at the Jefferson left a profound impression on me. Not that where I grew up in Queens was a great model of integration—it decidedly was not. As I noted earlier, there were very few blacks or other people of color in my neighborhood. However, the fact that some forms of real segregation were still alive and well in America was a shock to me. In New York, the concept of separate seating areas, separate facilities, etc. was anathema. But of course, where I lived, there would probably not have been any black folk in the neighborhood theater to begin with—because most neighborhoods were de facto segregated.

Old habits die hard—and that was the case in Charlottesville in the late 1960s. Buddy's Restaurant, located just north of the intersection of Emmet Street and University Avenue, had voluntarily shut down just before I arrived at UVA because the owner refused to integrate his establishment. There were other vestiges of the Old South that were also alive and well in Charlottesville when I first arrived, and, as we shall see, many would come under attack and disappear before I graduated—but that would not occur for a few more years.

## Down the Road

After my first week of classes, it was time to engage in the inevitable activity of any Wahoo seeking female companionship—the road-trip. Known as "going down the road" or more simply as "rolling" (as in, "We're rolling to Mary Wash tonight"), it was the natural consequence of attending an all-male college with no appreciable population of female students within thirty miles. This was not an unusual circumstance in the state of Virginia, where most institutions of higher learning were single sex or only nominally co-ed. Thus, I quickly learned that there were many potential destinations for the eager and willing young Cavalier. The issue then became—which school to roll to? In this regard, I was at a distinct disadvantage compared to many of my classmates. As an out-of-stater with no connections to the Commonwealth, I knew no women in residence at any of the numerous women's colleges throughout Virginia. As a result, I was pretty much at the mercy of some newfound friends who had girlfriends or former classmates at these schools. As I discussed the terrain with my classmates, I learned that the women's schools basically fell into three broad categories:

> 1.  The small liberal arts "refined" women's schools, highlighted by Hollins and Sweet Briar ("Sweets"), and also including Randolph-Macon Women's College ("Randy Mac" or "RMWC") and Mary Baldwin ("Mary Balls"). These were considered the "higher-end" destinations;
>
> 2.  The state teachers' colleges represented by Madison (the "Zone," now James Madison University), Radford and Longwood. These were considered the more "recreational" destinations; and
>
> 3.  Our "sister" school, Mary Washington ("Mary Wash"), which was considered fitting in somewhere between the other two categories.

There were other far-flung destinations, such as Sullins and Virginia Intermont in Bristol on the Tennessee border, or UNCG in Greensboro, North Carolina, or Hood and Goucher in Maryland. Hell, guys would drive anywhere for a putative decent date. But the above-mentioned eight schools tended to be the most popular road-trip destinations.

The choice of where to roll to depended upon a handful of factors, the most important being whether one of the road trip participants knew a woman at the destination who could arrange dates for the crew. In such a circumstance, you were relying on the judgment of your contact on the ground—a potentially dangerous situation. This problem was somewhat mitigated when you could get your hands on a "facebook" for the destination school in question. These were valuable commodities and were as studiously reviewed as any course textbook. Nevertheless, at least for my first year, the road trip was always an adventurous flight into the unknown.

The other major factor in determining a road trip destination was geography. The closest school was Mary Baldwin, about forty miles away in Staunton. However, a trip to Mary Balls necessitated a drive through the mountains on Route 250 (Interstate 64 had not been opened yet), which was two lanes for most of the trip. The ever-present evening fog drifting over the mountains, combined with the potential of bad weather, always made this drive somewhat dicey—particularly given the amount of alcohol usually consumed during any road trip. A trip to the Zone was also through the mountains, and a half hour beyond Staunton. Hollins, near Roanoke, was over 120 miles away and thus over a two-hour drive, making it almost prohibitive for a weeknight road trip unless special circumstances warranted it. Radford was another half hour beyond Hollins. Sweet Briar and Randy Mac in the Lynchburg vicinity, Longwood in Farmville and Mary Wash in Fredericksburg were closer, but still each over an hour away. Of course, all of this was academic first year before rush began, since you rarely had access to a car. My first road trip was made hitchhiking with a pal to Mary Wash. I remember it well because on the return trip to Charlottesville we were picked up by a truck manned by two characters right out of the famed novel and movie Deliverance. I still recall that as being a close call.

Having reached your destination, whichever one that might be, the course of events was pretty well determined by a number of factors. Was this a return visit to someone you had already met, or were you being fixed up? Were you in a large group or a small group? What was the weather like? The venue for the evening could range from a bar in Lynchburg, to a party in a motel room in Harrisonburg, to a blanket on a battlefield in Fredericksburg. In any event, most of the time it was a great deal of fun, if many times awkward, and generally the women were as happy to be there as we were—escaping from their convent as we were from our monastery.

In addition to seeking the comforts of cavorting with the opposite sex, a major objective of the road trip was often to find a date for the next "big weekend." As we will explore more fully later, much of the social life at UVA in the 1960s revolved around the party weekends in Charlottesville. And particularly for an out-of-state underclassman with few or no contacts at the women's colleges, the ability to actually meet someone beforehand whom you would like to spend a weekend with was a major windfall. The alternative was the dreaded weekend "blind date" —the lot of many a young Wahoo, but preferable to having no date at all for a big weekend, the ultimate social catastrophe.

While it is true that the road trip was primarily an attempt to acquire female companionship in some form, it also acted as a male bonding experience with your rolling buddies. The trip to and from the chosen destination was often as entertaining as the main event. The continuous banter and repartee, combined with the excitement and anticipation of the forthcoming encounter, made for an energized atmosphere—especially when fueled by the inevitable six packs that accompanied the journey. Obviously, it was not wise to be consuming a number of brews while driving long distances, often on narrow roads and through fog bound mountains, etc., but for whatever reason, no one really gave it much thought back then. The societal condemnation of drinking while driving was just not nearly as strong then as it has rightly become in more recent times. The wonder is not that the University lost a few students each year to drunk driving, but that we didn't lose more given the circumstances—and that no big deal was even made of it by the powers-that-be.

In any event, the ride back to Charlottesville was most often consumed by everyone sharing notes on the activities of the evening. It was the typical locker room nonsense, but it was these types of shared experiences that helped forge close friendships. By the time you made it back to the University, often well past midnight, the road oftentimes led to the two twenty-four-hour eateries located on the Corner, that stretch of retail shops and restaurants located on the northeast "corner" of the central Grounds.[19] The University Diner ("UD") and the White Spot fed many hungry and weary Wahoos at all hours of the night for decades.

The White Spot, presided over by the ever-present Henry, served up the famous "Gus Burger," a cheeseburger topped by a fried egg and fried onions. A truly hungry traveler could add an order of home fries—which appeared as a congealed mass of grease-inundated spuds. One can still visit the White Spot today on the Corner. Henry is long gone, the Gus Burger seems to have lost some of its zest and the Spot has grown in size, now offering table seating in addition to the counter seating only that existed in the sixties and seventies. In fact, it was the small size of the White Spot combined with its relatively limited menu that led many students to its roomier competitor farther east on the Corner beyond the railroad underpass.

*The Corner in the 1960's*

The UD[20] was my choice for late-night grunts. It was a tradition-ally configured diner, surrounded by large photos of famous UVA

---

19  Every UVA student is well acquainted with the Corner. There is no need to go into great detail discussing this beloved plot of land, since all anyone could ever want to know about the Corner is contained in the outstanding eponymous coffee table book by Coy Barefoot.

20  The UD's old location is now occupied by the Fig Bistro.

sports heroes such as "Bullet" Bill Dudley, Buzzy Wilkinson, and Jim Bakhtiar (the "Persian Prince"), and was tended to by the ever-loquacious mini-skirted Ethel. The UD's answer to the Gus Burger was its own "One-eyed Bacon Cheeseburger," which in essence was a Gus Burger minus the onions but plus a few strips of bacon. However, the pièce de résistance was the UD's famous "grills with." This concoction was a dietitian's nightmare—two glazed donuts, warmed up on the same grill with the burgers and bacon (the "grills") and then topped with two scoops of ice cream (the "with"). Given the imbibing on the way down the road and the artery-clogging eats on the return, it is amazing that so many of us survived these journeys.

Having detailed the nuances of going down the road, I wouldn't want one to think that I was by any means a road king. As far as I can recall, I probably traveled down the road around half a dozen times a year. Some of my more ambitious colleagues could rack up that total in a month. (Such a road warrior was often referred to as a "Road's Scholar.") In truth, I found the process awkward and not suited to my personality. It was similar in many ways to the bar scene in New York City that I encountered after leaving the University. You always felt as if you had to be "on" and selling yourself while making the most of the short time allotted to the encounter. There was nothing natural about it. There was precious little time to get to know the woman you were fixed up with or whom you met by chance. If you were lucky and there was some resulting mutual interest, the next step would be another road-trip rendezvous or an invitation to Charlottesville for a party weekend—which, as we shall see, also did not afford much of an opportunity for actually getting acquainted with your date. While I really did not focus on it at the time, in retrospect I came to realize how unnatural the whole system was. It surely would have been nice to be able to meet a woman in class or at an activity and get to know her as a person before pounding down a few beers or heading for the back seat of a car.

# The Largest Open Distillery in the Country

As I recall, I attended my first UVA football game on the Saturday following my first Friday night road trip. I put on my coat and tie and headed over to Scott Stadium with a bunch of my corridor buddies to see the Wahoos take on Wake Forest. I was then, and always have been, a big sports fan. Growing up in NYC, I had attended dozens of professional baseball, football, basketball, and hockey games. New Yorkers tend to take their sports seriously—but I soon learned that this was not the case at UVA in 1966.

The fact of the matter was that big-time sports were not part of the Virginia culture at that time. Other than football, few Wahoos attended sporting events. Basketball, which had recently moved from World War I-era Memorial Gymnasium to newly opened University Hall, might, on a very good night, attract a few thousand fans, and lacrosse might get a few hundred on a nice afternoon, but that was about it. And I soon learned that football, the flagship sport, was viewed more as a social event than a serious athletic contest. This attitude toward athletics permeated the University from the top down. Thus, UVA athletes tended to be treated as true student-athletes rather than as the quasi-professionals that has become the norm over the past few decades. In the McCormick Road dorms, the first-year football and basketball players were spread out amongst all the rest of their fellow students, not segregated in designated dorms or confined to separate dining facilities. As upperclassmen, athletes lived somewhat similar lives to other students—joined fraternities, served in student government, etc. Athletics tended to be an adjunct to their lives as students, rather than the other way around. A far cry from the world of today.

In any event, I digress from my initial trip to Scott Stadium—a mere five-minute walk from the first-year dorms. In 1966, Scott Stadium looked pretty much the same as it did when it first opened in October 1931 as a replacement for Lambeth Field.[21] Like much at UVA, little had changed in decades. Just as when constructed, the stadium had one lower deck, two open ended spaces beyond the goal posts on its east and west sides and a seating capacity of about twenty-five thousand. As we settled onto our benches, it soon became apparent that the football game itself basically served as a backdrop for another alcohol-sodden party. As the game was about to start, the Virginia Cavalier in full fig rode in on horseback waving his sword (an event that survives to this day, although the Cavalier was appropriately a student in those days), the half dozen or so male cheerleaders began jumping around with their megaphones, the band struck up Dixie and one of my colleagues produced his flask full of bourbon and suggested we all buy cups of Coke as mixers. And thus I learned that the most important accoutrement at a UVA football game was a hip flask.

In 1966, as is the case today, alcoholic beverages were prohibited from Scott Stadium. However, unlike at present, that prohibition was, as Hamlet said, "More honor'd in the breach than the observance." Most Wahoos entered the stadium with a flask full of bourbon or rum and left with an empty one. You see, every home football game was considered to be part of an ongoing party, due to the fact that each game was cause in and of itself for a "party weekend," which was the central focus of social life at all-male UVA (more on this shortly). Thus, as the game continued and flasks were emptied, the festivities mounted and the band would inevitably accompany the raucous singing of the various verses of the UVA drinking song.

Sitting at a UVA football game today, one will not hear the Virginia drinking song (a.k.a., "Rugby Road to Vinegar Hill") being sung. Not

---

21 Lambeth Field was constructed in the early part of the twentieth century as the primary venue for most UVA sports at the time. It was named after William Alexander Lambeth M.D., who served on the University faculty for forty years and was known as the "Father of Athletics" at the University. He is perhaps most famous for serving on the ICAA (the predecessor of the NCAA) Football Rules Committee, which in 1910 instituted new safety rules that are credited with saving football as an intercollegiate sport. The famous Lambeth Field "Colonnades" and stands can still be seen at UVA, but part of the field is now occupied by student apartments.

surprisingly, the changing attitudes toward drinking on Grounds have effectively consigned this song to the dustbins of history. For those not familiar with this anthem, the first and most famous verse is as follows:

> From Rugby Road to Vinegar Hill,
> We're gonna get drunk tonight.
> The faculty's afraid of us,
> They know we're in the right.
> So fill up your cups, your loving cups
> As full as full can be.
> And as long as love and liquor last,
> We'll drink to the U of V.
>
> Refrain:
> Oh, I think we need another drink. Hey!
> I think we need another drink. Hey!
> I think we need another drink…
> For the glory of the UVA.

*At Scott Stadium, Fall 1967*

As one can easily guess from the lyrics, this song has become musica non grata. And even more opprobrium would be heaped today on many of the subsequent verses, which even then were acknowledged to be sexist, bawdy and downright nasty. But one shouldn't think that your average Wahoo was really much more macho than the typical U.S. male. It must be remembered that this was the era of "Mad Men," where JFK and LBJ had turned the White House into veritable plea-sure palaces, where your male icon was the Marlboro Man, and where one of my law school classmates from Yale proudly noted that most Yalies aspired to be "MAPS Men" (the acronym standing for Money, Alcohol, Power, and Sex). That's the way it was in the 1960s—not many "sensitive" or "metrosexual" types to be found.

Lost in the revelry and merriment was the fact that Virginia actu-ally had a pretty good football team in 1966. This was quite surprising given that the Cavaliers had in the not-too-distant past recorded one of the most disgraceful extended records in the nation. Between 1953 and 1961, UVA had nine straight losing seasons with a combined win-loss record of 17-70. In the three-year period from 1958 to 1960, the Wahoos were a mind-numbing 1-29, including two back to back 0-10 records. However, by 1966 under new Coach George Blackburn, UVA was a competitive team led by two stars—one finishing his career and one just beginning his. Quarterback Bob Davis was the last of the great "triple threat" backs. In his last year at UVA in 1966, Davis was to lead the ACC in total offense and passing yards. Playing behind him in his first year of varsity,[22] tailback Frank Quayle as a rookie would lead the ACC in scoring and all-purpose yards. Quayle was the most explosive offensive player I have ever seen at UVA (and I have followed UVA football closely since that first game in 1966) and was named the ACC Player of the Year and the conference's overall athlete in 1968. The Wahoos would end the 1966 football season with a 4-6 record, improve to 5-5 in 1967 and have an outstanding season in 1968, when

---

22  At this time, first-year men still played on freshman teams. Freshman athletes were first allowed to play varsity football in 1972.

they were 7-3 with one of the best offensive teams in Cavalier history (scoring more than 40 points in half their games). Indeed, my friend Andy Selfridge, who was a linebacker on the team, told me that following Virginia's 63-47 home victory over Tulane, Coach Blackburn said to the Tulane coach as they were shaking hands after the high scoring affair, "I'm afraid we set college football defenses back a hundred years today."

Well, we won that opening game against Wake 24-10, and I walked back to the dorms elated both in having seen a good football game and having participated in a mass communal party that made me happy to be a Wahoo. The Cavalier culturization process was in full force.

*Frank Quayle busting through*

## The Hair Fair

Shortly before fraternity rush began, when most of us were still trying to find ways to occupy our evenings when not studying, one of my locally based classmates with access to a car asked if I would like to accompany a group going to the "Hair Fair." Not surprisingly, my retort was something to the effect of, "What the hell is the Hair Fair?" I was informed forthwith that it was the county fair held at the polo grounds out north of town. Although there were no county fairs in NYC, I had been to the Orange County Fair a few times while working during the summers in the Catskill Mountains—kids rides, games of skill and chance, cotton candy, etc. That did not seem to be a particularly exciting way to spend a Friday night. I was therefore about to respond that I wasn't interested, when I thought to ask, "Why is it called the Hair Fair?" Well, that was the magic question. A sly smile crossed my colleague's face, and he said I should let that be a surprise, while assuring me I would have a great time. So without other enticing options, I piled into the car with a few other fellows and headed north on Route 29 to the polo grounds.

We arrived at the fair and, at first, it appeared to be exactly what I had imagined—families walking around with small children, high school sweethearts hand in hand, merry-go-rounds, ring-the-bottle, American Legion types collecting tickets, the pervasive smell of popcorn. I couldn't understand what we were doing there, which I verbalized to my friend. He just said, "Follow me." So we walked through the fair toward a tent in the very back. As we approached the tent, I could hear loud music thumping from within. A fellow out front collected our payment to enter and pulled aside a canvas doorway. Once inside, I was immediately enveloped by a dense fug of cigarette smoke, alcohol, and sweat. And what I saw through this malodorous smog stopped me in my tracks.

Up on a stage were three women, buck naked, gyrating in a fashion that would have put Gypsy Rose Lee to shame. Well, my jaw just about hit the ground. Here I was, in the South, amidst a family-friendly county fair, and viewing the most lewd and nasty spectacle I had ever seen. I could hardly believe my eyes. In NYC at that time, the most ribald movies on 42$^{nd}$ Street would barely deserve an "R" rating today—and this was taking place in a part of the country where the only things you could hear on the radio on Sunday were sermons and hymns. I stood there witnessing amazing things being done with cigarettes and ping pong balls, and as we moved closer to the stage, I can remember my friend warning us—don't get too close to the stage if you're wearing glasses, because you will have your spectacles cleaned in a manner that you've never seen before.

I later learned that the Hair Fair was shut down a few years afterwards. But that was a hell of an introduction to a distinct segment of Southern culture.

## *Rush*

And then there was the proverbial elephant in the room. I knew even before coming down to Charlottesville that the decision of whether to join a fraternity would be an important one. However, I did not realize how important that decision would be until I arrived on Grounds. It did not take long to realize that at a relatively small all-men's school, located in a small town over a hundred miles from the closest major metropolis, you needed some type of independent organization to manufacture much-needed leisure time diversions. In essence, you had to create your own fun—and no entity did that better than the fraternity system. The fraternities not only provided an instant coterie of fifty or so guys to pal around with, to dine with, to go down the road with, etc., but also very significantly provided an established party venue for big weekends—which were the lifeblood of UVA social life. In addition, it also became apparent relatively quickly that the fraternities were a key entrée into most of the major student activities around Grounds. The fact was that in 1966, although fraternity men represented less than fifty percent of the undergraduate student population, they controlled virtually every important organ of student life—the Honor Committee, the Judiciary Committee, the Student Council, the University Union, *The Cavalier Daily*, the *University of Virginia Magazine*, and the *Corks and Curls*. Thus, within a few weeks, the realities of life at UVA confirmed my initial inclination to engage in fraternity rush.

In the late 1960s, rush began in early October of first semester and lasted for approximately six weeks. This is in marked contrast to the rush calendar that exists presently and that has existed for some time at UVA. The powers-that-be at the University moved rush to second semester well over a decade ago and the length of the rush period has consistently shrunk to the point that it now lasts for only two weeks. In my opinion, neither of these material changes were wise ones, but they exemplify a decades-old trend both nationally and at UVA to diminish "Greek" life. I will note right up front that my fraternity experience played an extremely important role in my life at UVA. I feel comfortable in saying that in no way would my experience at the University have been as rich and rewarding without it. But more on that later.

Rush began on October 5 with dorm visits. In the army, we called this a "recky," or more formally, a reconnaissance. Each fraternity split up its membership into teams, who then had a certain amount of time to visit with first-years in their dorm rooms. In essence, the frats were getting the "lay of the land." The decision on which students to visit was based on a number of factors, including prior relationships from high schools or hometowns, information gathered from dorm counselor members of the fraternity and a study of the first-year facebook. Interactions with first-years outside of formal rush events were forbidden—known as "dirty rush"—and such prohibition tended to be strictly enforced.

So the early October dorm visits marked the first-year men's initial real contacts with fraternity members. For those interested in rush, the process was no small endeavor. In 1966, there were thirty-one fraternities at UVA—and not surprisingly, each one had its own distinct character and reputation. Thus, you had your preppy houses, jock houses, student leader houses and Southern houses; more broadly, the fraternities were informally viewed reputation-wise as top-tier, middle-tier and lower-tier houses. But for me, in actuality, the process was much less complicated. While there were thirty-one fraternities, there were three "Jewish" houses (AEPi, PhiEp, and ZBT) and, de facto, that was my playing field. There was always the exception that proved the rule—in

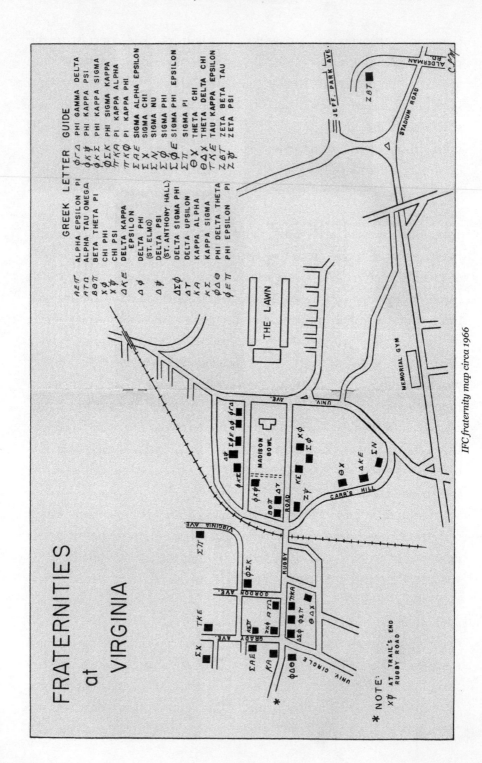

*IFC fraternity map circa 1966*

1966 one of the top-tier "preppy" houses pledged a Jewish student—but ninety-nine percent of Jewish fraternity members were in the three Jewish houses. Perhaps that was partly by choice, but in my experience most of it was due to lack of opportunity. The fact of the matter was that, with rare exceptions, most of the non-Jewish fraternities did not even attempt to rush Jewish students. Along with most everything else at UVA, this would change before I graduated in 1970, but in 1966, the walls were still intact.

Dorm visits were a fascinating introduction to rush; sitting in your dorm room in your coat and tie, waiting for the knock on the door and hoping for someone to show some interest. That first night, I did get visited by the three Jewish fraternities as well as a few of the lower-tier houses. My roommate, Bronson Percival, was visited by many more, which didn't surprise me a bit, with a moniker like that and his being a Virginian. However, it was all lost on him, as he had no interest in rushing. The next day, dorm visits were the main topic of conversation among the first-year class and a few amusing stories arose. The one I remember best was about the one house whose members checked the sports coat labels in the open dorm room closets to see how refined (or wealthy) the candidate was. Well, good luck to anyone who wanted to look in my closet and check out my coats—no Brooks Brothers or J. Press to be found there. In fact, many of my coats were purchased wholesale and had no label at all.

After dorm visits, the next event was "open rush" house visitation. During the first round of "smokers" (non-party-weekend, evening rush functions) any first-year man could visit any house. Though I knew I would be focusing on only three houses, I figured this was a great opportunity to meet a lot of people and see the insides of many of the much-vaunted old line fraternity houses. For those not familiar with UVA, most of the fraternity houses are clustered north of the Rotunda, either adjacent or in proximity to two roads—the famed Rugby Road and Madison Lane. Many of these houses, particularly those closest to the main Grounds, are picture-book Greek Revival-style mansions. The beauty of these buildings, one next to another, bordering the large expanse of Mad Bowl,[23] was and is today exceptional. For a kid from Queens, it was like I had been transported to a collegiate Disneyland, and I meant to make the most of it. So I donned my three-piece suit (just a coat and tie was insufficient for the first formal smoker) and headed out for a new adventure.

My objective was to visit as many houses as possible in the three or so hours available. Each house was alive with music, chatter, cigarette smoke and the ever-present keg of beer. As you walked into each fraternity, the pattern was the same—a quick introduction, a cup of brew placed in your hand, followed by some brief or lengthy conversations, depending upon whether there was mutual interest between the brotherhood and yourself. Since I already knew that in my case mutual interest was pretty much limited to three fraternities, my visits to other houses were relatively brief experiences, more to expand my horizons than anything else. However, you did have one or two cups of beer at each frat you visited, so that by the fourth or fifth house, things started to get a bit hazy. Nevertheless, there was one incident that still stands out in my memory from that first night of open rush.

While wandering up Mad Lane and Rugby Road along with hundreds of other wide-eyed first-year men, I bumped into the only classmate whom I had known prior to coming down to UVA. Joel Stone was also to my knowledge one of only two other public high school kids from NYC in our class. We had attended the same summer camp a few years earlier. So the other Joel and I decided to visit a number of houses together. As we walked up Rugby Road, one of the first houses we visited was Zeta Psi. The Zete house had a well-founded reputation as a top-tier fraternity full of student leaders. We walked up the steps, past the large white columns, and introduced ourselves to the brother at the front door. It soon became apparent that the fellow realized who he was dealing with (two Joel's from NYC), and it wasn't two Woodberry

---

23   Mad Bowl (short for Madison Bowl) is a large, rectangular, open, grassy sunken field, normally used for athletic activities, which is bordered on the west by Rugby Road, the east by Madison Lane, the south by Madison Hall and the north by the Phi Kappa Psi fraternity house.

Forest grads. He smiled and said something like, "Nice to meet you. Come on in and have a beer. But you know that this is the Zete house," (pause), "I think you guys are looking for the ZBT house." While I knew the lay of the land and never expected to be actively rushed by Zete, I had not anticipated the reality to be so directly thrust in my face. In today's world, I guess that would be considered to be at least a "micro-aggression," if not perhaps a "macro-aggression." But in 1966, such sensitivities were not quite so acute, and concepts of "victimization" not yet fully developed. So we went into the Zete house, looked around, had yet another beer and quickly departed.

While the event obviously left an impression on me, I really did not let it bother me much. The fact of the matter was that the Zete house was indeed an excellent group of guys, and by the time I graduated, I had numerous friends who were members. And while the brother at the door would probably today be mandated for "sensitivity" training, he actually had a point. Even if the exclusionary walls had been magically removed, the Zete house was not the right fit for me in 1966. And if the fraternity experience is to be a positive one, it is so important to find the right fit.

After open rush was over, the rest of rush activities were by invitation only. These activities consisted of lunches, dinners, smokers, and "combo" parties (parties during party weekends). I was fortunate to get invitations from all three of the Jewish fraternities, and thus spent the next few weeks getting to know the brothers at these houses as well as my fellow classmates rushing those houses. Significantly, it was as important, if not more so, to meet those other first-years who might be in your pledge class as it was meeting the brothers already in the fraternity. While I liked the brothers at all three houses, as the weeks and events passed, I started gravitating toward the AEPi house. I just felt more comfortable there—and, fortunately, the feeling was mutual. Thus, with about two weeks remaining in rush, I was asked to "commit" to AEPi. By committing, I was guaranteed a bid in return for my agreeing to both stop rushing other houses and assist the brothers in rushing other uncommitted first-years. I was quite flattered by the proposal, accepted, and spent the last few weeks of rush helping to convince other classmates who were on the fence to choose AEPi.

Rush culminated with bid Sunday on November 13. The fraternities delivered bids to the McCormick Road dorms during the day, such bids to be returned to the house a few hours later. Our new pledge class had decided to meet at a designated place in the dorm complex and return the bids as a group. As it turned out, we had quite a large class, about twenty-five fellows, and I remember well marching together up Rugby Road shouting A-E-Pi, A-E-Pi, howling as we passed the PhiEp house, making the right turn on Grady Avenue and being greeted in front of the house by a gauntlet of the brothers cheering us on. We rushed through the gauntlet and into the house to be greeted and feted as the new life blood of the organization. Of course, once the festivities of bid Sunday were over, pledging began—and that is another story.

And what an extraordinary pledge class we had. After the dust settled and a few fellows dropped out, we wound up with twenty-two members in our class. Interestingly, what on the surface appeared to be a relatively homogeneous pool of students was in actuality a very diverse group of guys. We were from ten states, split about fifty-fifty from the North and South; from big cities (e.g., NYC, Cleveland, Boston), mid-size cities (e.g.,Memphis, Norfolk, Chattanooga) and small towns (e.g., Booneville, Mississippi; Painter, Virginia); we were wealthy, middle class and on student aid; we were liberals, moderates and conservatives. Yes, we were all Jewish, but I quickly learned that, just as was the case for the population at large, there tended to be significant differences between the Jews from the North and from the South and "big-city" Jews and "small-town" Jews. But most of all, this was an incredibly talented group of guys that would produce six Phi Beta Kappa's and some of the top student leaders of the class of 1970. Indeed, it was never boring walking into the house.

Looking back with decades of hindsight, I realize how fortunate I was to have made the choice I did. My decision to join AEPi was as important of a decision as I would make during my years as an undergraduate. For the next four years, that house would be my home and the pledges and brothers my family. As the years passed and I became involved in numerous activities around the Grounds, expanded my horizons and made numerous great friends outside AEPi, the house was still my "comfort zone"—a place I could always return to for company and friendship. I ate most of my meals there, and it was my home base for parties and the venue of hundreds of bull sessions and maybe even a few serious discussions. It was a place where you learned to get along with people of other backgrounds and viewpoints. Not everyone there would be your good friend or to your taste, but you learned to tolerate them because they were your "brothers." I can't even begin to imagine what life would have been like without it.

## *Big Weekends*

In many ways, the "big weekends" at UVA in the 1960s were as much a part of the fabric of the Old U as coats and ties and the Honor System. The four major and two minor big party weekends were the linchpins of social life at the University. Each semester had two major and one minor "big weekends." In the fall, the majors were Homecomings (October) and Openings (November) and the minor was Christmas Parties (December); in the spring the majors were Midwinters (February) and Easters (April) and the minor was IFC Weekend (March).[24] It is difficult in today's world to imagine the social significance of these whirlwind festivities at an isolated male university. At today's very coed UVA, continuous social interaction takes place at various venues—dorms, bars, apartments, fraternity houses, even libraries. My understanding is that social functions now start on Wednesday evening and continue through Saturday night. No such luck for the old boys back at the U in the 1960s. Except for those few Road's Scholars who rolled during the week, social interaction was confined to weekends—and for most, not every weekend

---

24  In the fall, a home football game weekend which did not coincide with a "big weekend" was also cause for group parties-- just not on the same level as a big weekend.

at that. And even when you were down the road on a weekend, the time with one's date was for a few hours at best. Thus, the party weekend represented an attempt to cram weeks' worth of socializing into two short days—resulting in excesses of every kind.

*"I Promised Mother Not To Drink Or Smoke. What Else Is There To Do?"*
*Front page of The Cavalier Daily, Openings 1966—a sign of the times*

The 1966 *Cavalier Daily* orientation issue described the big weekend as "two-and-a-half days of merry-making bordering on debauchery" that was meant to make up "for any lack of feminine pulchritude around the Grounds." The festivities would begin Friday night and continue unabated until Sunday. The most consequential opening event was the hopeful arrival of one's date. This generally occurred on Friday afternoon or evening—although longstanding girlfriends might arrive on Thursday night. And they arrived by every means of transportation available—cars, trains, buses, and planes. The Grounds, normally bereft of "feminine pulchritude," was suddenly inundated with it. And they came from far and wide—from the usual suspects like Sweet Briar, Randy Mac, Mary Wash, the Zone, etc. as well as from just about any school on the East Coast and in the South. UVA party weekends were definitely a magnet and a "thing to do." Also, especially for the underclassmen who had not had the opportunity to establish a beachhead at any of the women's schools, a big weekend was an opportunity to invite one's "hometown honey" to see the Grounds and experience the U.

As noted previously, in the social order of things, having a date for a big weekend was a top priority. No date, no festivities. Given this situation, it is not surprising that some interesting scenarios ensued. One of the most fascinating in retrospect was the multitude of "fix-ups" and "first time after a road trip dates" flooding into Charlottesville, thus throwing together for an entire weekend two people who either didn't know or barely knew each other. The dynamics were potentially explosive and often resulted in behavior that was less than exemplary. An example was the "showdown" at the bus station. Every time I drive by the Greyhound bus station on West Main Street (which was the Trailways station in the 1960s), a smirk inadvertently crosses my face, because back in the day, that bus station on the Friday night of a big weekend was the scene of anticipation, expectation, exhilaration, or frustration, as scores of Wahoos waited for the buses to roll in from Lynchburg, Roanoke, Harrisonburg, Fredericksburg and other points north, south, east and west.[25] Many of these young Cavaliers were waiting for a first glimpse of a date with whom they had been fixed up or trying to remember what one's date looked like after having met her only once on a road trip while in the haze of a six pack. I stood in those shoes a number of times my first and second year, and I can tell you that the rumbling in the pit of your stomach as you waited for the bus door to open matched that of opening the envelope with your semester grades or waiting for your draft lottery number to be plucked from the basket. This socially unnatural scenario resulted on occasion in the infamous bus station desertions. While I never witnessed one personally, the stories were too legion to be pure fabrications. In such situa-

25  The area in front of the Rotunda on University Avenue was also a final stop for buses coming in from some of the women's colleges.

tions, the Wahoo in question when having his proposed date for the weekend pointed out to him, would do an about-face and bolt from the premises. Reprehensible behavior? Absolutely. Ungentlemanly? For sure! But given the prospects of spending the next thirty-six hours or so with someone you didn't want to be with—somewhat understandable.

Another legacy of this distinctly strange manner of dating was the practice employed by friends, acquaintances, fraternity brothers or just about anybody else of "snaking" others' dates. In common parlance, to "snake" a date was to relieve your fellow student of his partner, either willingly or unwillingly. Because of the lack of long-term attachment between many, if not most, of the couples on any given big weekend, this practice occurred rather frequently. In fact, some fellows would purposely not get a date for the weekend with the anticipation of snaking one during the festivities. Other potential "snakers" included those who could not arrange a date prior to the weekend, those who were "shot down" unexpectedly by their prospective date just before the weekend (the female version of the bus-stop desertion) and those who would dump their date during the weekend for a better prospect. It all sounds so cruel and thoughtless—and it was. But in retrospect, it was just another natural consequence of the unnatural social situation of being at an isolated single-sex institution.

Once your date actually arrived in Charlottesville, it was often your responsibility to find a place to house her. One must remember that in 1966, students living in University housing or in the fraternity houses were not allowed to have women in their rooms.

The issue was fairly well defined if your date was from one of the Commonwealth's high-echelon private women's colleges such as Hollins, Sweets, or Randy Mac. Through the late 1960s, these young ladies were required to stay in "approved housing" accommodations when traveling to UVA for a weekend. Each of these schools had a list of private residences (most maintained by elderly women) that were "approved" for overnight stays. The female student was required to sign in and out and there were mandatory curfews. The concept was sort of a residential chastity belt. Of course, there were many tales of how these strictures were circumvented, and I'm not sure how rigorously enforced these rules were, but there was no doubt that the approved housing situation put some crimps into one's social flexibility. On the other hand, if your date was not from one of the relatively small group of refined women's colleges, the answer was your own apartment, a friend's apartment or one of the many motels in the vicinity. The Charlottesville hospitality industry did a booming business on big weekends.

Your date having arrived and settled in, it was time for the partying to begin. In actuality, the activities for a big weekend were rather formulaic. The festivities revolved around University-sponsored events and fraternity parties. The University-sponsored events were concerts on Friday and Saturday nights, and in the fall, football games Saturday afternoons. The Friday night event was called a "dance," but in essence was a seatless concert held in Memorial Gym. The Friday evening musical group was generally a second-class act when compared to the top card that played on Saturday night at University Hall.

The Saturday evening concert was usually led by a top nationally renowned group with a warm-up group to open. I remember well my first concert at U Hall—the Four Tops and Jr. Walker and the All Stars. I was astonished that a small venue like Charlottesville could attract such marquee acts. But attract them we did—and during my years at Virginia I saw most of the outstanding musical acts of the day— the Temptations, James Brown, Smokey Robinson, Sam & Dave, the Beach Boys, Wilson Pickett, Janis Joplin and Peter, Paul & Mary, to name just a few. Music was a big thing in Charlottesville in the 1960s. You not only had the numerous concerts on party weekends, there were also live bands at the fraternity houses for all big weekends. And in 1966 at UVA, music pretty much meant soul music, with an occasional splash of folk.

Before I went to to UVA, most of the music my friends and I listened to encompassed the British Invasion (the Beatles, the Rolling Stones, the Animals), the California sound (the Beach Boys, the Mamas and Papas, Sonny & Cher) and the new sounds of folk rock (the Lovin' Spoonful, the Byrds, the Association). To the extent that we listened to soul music, it was pretty much the recent introduction of the Motown sound as exemplified by the Supremes, the Temptations, the Four Tops, and Smokey Robinson. But at UVA, soul was king. And it wasn't just the sanitized soul music of Motown trying to appeal to a broad market; it was also the more authentic soul music exemplified by the Memphis sound to be found on the Stax and Atlantic labels. Sure, we listened to the Motown groups; but as popular, or even more so, were the Memphis sounds of Wilson Pickett, Otis Redding, Aretha Franklin, Sam & Dave, Carla Thomas, Percy Sledge, and, of course, the "King of Soul," James Brown. This was a more raw, visceral sound—not a lot of sanitization going on there. In order to appreciate this genre, one only has to look at some of the titles to popular cuts of that period—Sam & Dave's "Hold On, I'm Comin'," Johnny Jackson's "Who's Making Love to Your Old Lady," Wilson Pickett's "What's Under That Dress."[26] The above different sounds of soul were what one more likely than not would be hearing at U Hall, Mem Gym or along Rugby Road and Mad Lane emanating from the frat houses. It always amazed me as such a contradiction—that in a culture that was still basically segregated, the blacker the music, the more it was loved.

While the University-sponsored events were enjoyable, the real heart and soul of the big weekend festivities were the fraternity parties, which in 1966 were still basically open functions. Most of the fraternities had parties on both Friday and Saturday nights; and on Openings and Easters, there were also parties on Sunday afternoons. Virtually all the fraternities had live music Saturday night and many did Friday night as well. For those who never participated in the pre-coeducation big weekend extravaganzas, it is difficult to effectively describe the total experience: hundreds of couples walking along Rugby Road and Mad

---

26   And there were also the ever-popular regional soul bands. Two were from Tidewater, Virginia—Bill Deal and the Rondells, the kings of "blue-eyed" soul ("I've Been Hurt," "May I") and Bob Marshall and the Crystals ("She Shot a Hole in My Soul"). And for pure raunch, there was Doug Clark and the Hot Nuts.

Lane, arm in arm, with drink cups or cigarettes in their free hands, music blaring from each of the fraternity houses, party rooms filled with the pounding sensual rhythms of the soul bands, the pervasive smell of smoke, beer, perfume and sweat, and the flowing hormones palpable in the air. Couples grinding and making out to a slow dance ballad or crazy Cavs "gatoring" on the dance floor to the frenzied sounds of "Soul Man" or "Midnight Hour" surrounded by cheering guys and giggling gals.[27] If you ever saw the 1970s classic, Animal House, then you may have some idea of what these parties were like (sans togas). For that matter, there is actually quite a bit in Animal House that approximated life at UVA in the 1960s—more fact than fiction.

*Big weekend party at the AEPi house 1966*

The pièce de résistance of the big weekend was the Sunday afternoon grain party. These parties were often joint fraternity parties, particularly on Easters Weekend, when the weather was conducive to outdoor festivities. Indoors or outdoors, joint or solo, these parties were

---

27  "Gatoring" is a particularly Southern form of horizontal dancing where the dancer writhes on the ground in a decidedly erotic fashion.

raucous and outlandish and a fitting end to a big weekend.

For the uninitiated, grain alcohol is a form of pure alcohol. When not being imbibed, it can be used to run a tractor or take the varnish off your old furniture. Of course, being 190 proof, it was not to be consumed on its own. Rather, depending on how potent you wanted the brew to be, it was combined with a mixer at a ratio of four-to-one to six-to-one. The mixers of choice were fruit punches, the most popular at that time being Hawaiian Punch or Hi-C. The grape-flavored punches were often used, giving the resulting beverage the alliterative name of "purple passion." The concoction was most often mixed by the house brewmaster in large plastic garbage pails. The forty-eight-ounce mixer cans were often used as goblets for the potent brew. Those who could not get their hands on a can had to settle for mere plastic or paper cups.

*The detritus of a big weekend party*

The UVA grain parties were legendary—and I don't mean to romanticize the excesses that were attendant to them—only to tell it like it was. By late Sunday afternoon, there was nary a sober person in sight, male or female. I don't know how many of the women made it back home. A large proportion of young Wahoos were either passed out, wandering around sputtering more gibberish than usual or spilling their guts into any convenient receptacle. Not many were in any condition to drive or deliver their dates to the appropriate bus, train, or ride home.

The extraordinary amounts of alcohol consumed during big weekends shines a light on the very relevant question: how bad was the drinking problem at UVA at this time? The fact that periodic excessive drinking occurred is without doubt. On the other hand, such excesses were mostly confined to a relatively limited number of events—party weekends and road trips. Sure, one might have a beer down on the Corner with dinner, or share a bunch of Rolling Rock "pony" bottles with your buddies while listening to a sporting event on a Saturday afternoon, or hit the fraternity beer machine while watching the tube late at night, but in my experience, rarely was hard alcohol or significant amounts of beer consumed other than at the limited coed social events. For whatever reason (and I'm sure a psychologist would have a field day with the issue), many Wahoos felt that they had to be fortified by drink when interacting with the opposite sex. Indeed, one of my classmates recently said to me that he couldn't remember ever being sober when he was with a woman during our time at the University. An exaggeration perhaps, but probably not a great one. Here was another legacy of the absence of coeducation and the lack of a normal atmosphere for social interaction between the sexes.

The culmination of the big weekend culture at UVA was the Sunday afternoon Easters Weekend party of 1976. As the years went by, these festivities had become increasingly centered on Mad Bowl, as thousands of people, students and non-students, filled the rectangular depression to listen to live music and imbibe excessively. By the time I graduated in 1970, the tradition of hosing down the slopes of Mad Bowl and creating massive mudslides had been initiated. With each passing year, the numbers attending the spectacle increased and the mayhem intensified. By 1976, it was estimated that fifteen thousand people crowded into the bowl, and participants later commented that it resembled a Charlottesville "Woodstock." UVA administrators had apparently been looking for a reason to shut down the increasingly out-of-control merriment, and they seemed to have found one in the infamous dorm floods that followed the 1976 shenanigans. Apparently numerous first-year students were so full of mud that the newly renovated McCormick Road dorms were flooded by mud-clogged drains as the students attempted to disengage themselves from the muck in the showers. As a result, 1976 was the last year that Easters parties were held in Mad Bowl, and by 1982, Easters as a big weekend was history. Openings and Midwinters continued for a period, but they too shortly faded into the annals of UVA lore.

There is little doubt that the big weekend syndrome at UVA was very much a product of the University being both an isolated all-male institution and a paradigm of the Southern party culture. With the advent of coeducation and the death of the Old U ethic, it was only natural that big weekends would disappear into the mists along with coats and ties and road trips. Even when these party weekends were in full bloom, there was a recognition that they were part of an atavistic way of life. *The Cavalier Daily* expressed it well in its fall 1967 Openings Weekend issue: "The cares of the world are traded for however brief a period for a bottle of Scotch and a girl from Hollins. Not a bad deal at that... Social life at the University has retained a certain 1920—or even 1820—rakishness about it, and John Held or Scott Fitzgerald—or even Beau Brummel—would feel right at home."

~~~~~

The first big weekend I attended after rush was over was Openings in November 1966. The *CD* headlines announced: "Folk Songs, Football Featured in Openings Revelry. Multitudes of Females Descend on University for Wahoos Festivities." The event I remember most about that weekend was the bonfire in the fraternity Quad[28] that consumed a piano, a door, a bench and a chair from two fraternities. I recall it well because it was an unusual event at that time. Things were somewhat wild in 1966, but not as wild as they would become later. The reason for that I believe is that in 1966, if your behavior was out of line, you had to answer to the most formidable administrator in my memory at UVA—Dean Runk.

## *Dean Runk*

For all those who remember the autocratic character of Dean Wormer in Animal House, well, we had our own version of sorts at UVA in 1966. B.F.D. Runk was Dean of the University (a title that has not existed since his retirement), and he was one of those larger-than-life characters that strode the Grounds in the 1960s. Yes, B.F.D. were his actual initials (Benjamin Franklin Dewees) and not an acronym. It has been said that while he was dean, from 1959 to 1968, he in effect ran the University. It certainly seemed that way from a student's point of view. He planted a firm fist on every aspect of student life.

Dean Runk first arrived at UVA as a student in 1925. He received his B.S. degree in 1929, his M.S. in 1930, and his Ph.D. in biology in 1939. He became a full professor of biology at the University and began his administrative duties as an advisor to students in 1955. In 1956, he became registrar and in 1959 Dean of the University. In this latter position, he was in charge of all aspects of student life, and he filled this responsibility in a very hands-on manner. Dean Runk was probably able to exercise even more authority than normal due to the fact his appointment as dean in 1959 coincided with the inauguration of a new young president of the University—Edgar F. Shannon. The personalities of the two could not have been more different. Dean Runk had a big, bold personality—a force of nature in his own right. On the

---

28  The Quad is an area on Rugby Road just north of the art museum and across from Mad Bowl that is surrounded on three sides by grand brick white-pillared fraternity houses—Kappa Sigma, Chi Phi and, at that time, Sigma Phi.

other hand, Edgar Shannon was a Tennyson scholar, relatively quiet and contemplative. I knew them both—they were both wonderful men, but very different in their approaches to leadership.

*Dean B.F.D. Runk*

Dean Runk's ability to strongly assert his views on University life during his deanship was thus not surprising—and his views were strictly and unadulteratedly Old U. He was a firm believer in coats and ties and the Honor System, was unabashedly opposed to coeducation and was a stickler for gentlemanly behavior in all its manifestations. Woe unto those who displayed behavior unbecoming a Virginia Gentleman and faced the wrath of Dean Runk. Fortunately, I never had to appear before Dean Runk for an alleged transgression, but I knew a number who had. It was not a warm and fuzzy experience. Apparently, the best out-comes were achieved when one came appropriately attired (coat and tie, socks, laced-up shoes) and demonstrated heartfelt remorse. Even then, punishments could be draconian—probation, suspension and even dis-missal. He strictly enforced written rules and regulations and just as strictly enforced the unwritten rules of gentlemanly behavior. I don't think Dean Runk would have tolerated for a minute a Virginia student physically mistreating a woman or placing a "roofie" in her drink. He ruled with an iron glove that would not be possible in today's world of helicopter parents and omnipresent litigation.

I think it is safe to say that the 1966-1967 school year was the last true period of the Old U—and in fact it was the last year that Dean Runk ruled the Grounds as a monolith. With change in the air, it was announced in October 1967 that Robert Canevari was appointed Assistant Dean of the University to "lighten" Dean Runk's load. And shortly thereafter, in May 1968, it was simultaneously announced that Alan Williams was appointed Dean of Student Affairs and that Dean Runk would retire as of June. It was the end of an era. *The Cavalier Daily* clearly recognized the significance of Dean Runk's departure, asserting that his retirement "means the withdrawal from the forefront of one of the most strenuous defenders of the 'faith' of the University of Virginia now in residence in the University Community."

While Dean Runk stepped down as dean in 1968, he continued as Grand Marshall of the University, a position he held until the fall of 1976. As Grand Marshall, Dean Runk led academic processions down the Lawn while carrying the University mace. A whole generation of Wahoos will remember following in his footsteps as they too marched down the Lawn to receive the "honor of honors."[29] B.F.D. Runk passed away in 1994 after an almost-seven-decade love affair with the University of Virginia. He had never married—UVA was the love of his life.

Before moving on, I want to leave you with a Dean Runk story. It may be an apocryphal one—I did not witness it and have not seen it in

---

29  Another UVA term for a degree from the University.

writing anywhere. But I heard it as a student and from others since—and it so perfectly encapsulates the man. The story goes that a mother of a student visited Dean Runk to complain about her son, a member of Zeta Psi fraternity, having been branded as part of his brotherhood journey. Dean Runk sat politely behind his desk, not saying a word, as the woman fulminated about this abhorrent behavior. When she was finished, Dean Runk calmly pushed back his chair, stood up, took off his jacket, rolled up his shirt sleeve, smiled, and produced for the lady his own Zete brand mark which he had proudly worn for decades—end of story. And that was Dean Runk—true story or not.

## *Pledging*

As soon as rush was over, the proverbial "bloom was off the rose," and pledging began for those who had decided to enter the Greek world. The first and perhaps most significant characteristic that distinguished pledging in the late 1960s from pledging today was the length of time. Currently, pledging lasts for about two months in the spring of one's first year; back in the day, the pledge period lasted for almost a full year. It began in November of your first year and ended at the beginning of the fall semester of second year. The brothers would probably have liked to extend it even further, but they needed you in the brotherhood for the beginning of the next rush cycle. For me (and I believe most others in the process), pledging occupied much of my time outside of the classroom and library. Besides pledge duties, pledging required being at the house and getting to know the fraternity and its members. Some critical of fraternities might see this as a very limiting situation, but that was not my experience. In fact, the opportunity of getting to know rather quickly sixty or so fellows from all over the country, first to fourth years, with a wide range of interests and personalities, was a very broadening experience. Indeed, an experience that probably could not have occurred outside the fraternity system.

In retrospect, probably the most important part of beginning pledging was starting to eat virtually all my meals at the house. In the 1960s, all fraternities had cooks and all pledges and brothers were expected to eat at the house. At the AEPi house, we had lunch and dinner served every weekday and lunch on Saturdays. Most members showed up for lunch daily, even though the house's location on Grady Avenue was a fair distance from the Central Grounds, and generally all were present for dinner. Just like in old-fashioned America, where dinner time was the one opportunity to get the whole family together and socially interact (those were pre-iPhone days), so was the case with the fraternity. While partying and going down the road together were certainly bonding experiences, the real place you got to know your fellow pledges and brothers was at mealtimes. I am not sure when most fraternities at UVA stopped having their own cooks and eating meals together every day, but I believe losing that daily interaction has taken something material from the fraternity experience.

In addition, the food was actually pretty good at the Pi lodge. Our cook, Mary Fortune, served a varied menu that featured some fine Southern cuisine as well as the standard meat and potatoes. In retrospect, this was amazing given the low cost of our meals, even for that time period. A lot of this could be attributed to the astute oversight of our kitchen managers (not bad experience for an undergraduate to be running a daily meal service for sixty people—thanks Messrs. Pape and Kaplan). Of course, there were places where corners were cut— who can forget the reject pot pies purchased for pennies at the Morton facility in Crozet. You stuck your fork in the crust and the whole pie collapsed. But as a whole, the food was good and plentiful. This was especially beneficial in a Charlottesville that did not offer much in terms of dining opportunities. This was particularly true on Grounds, where in 1966 there was only one major dining option—the cafeteria at Newcomb Hall (the student union), which served institutional cuisine the likes of which I did not encounter again until basic training at Fort Dix. The only source of food in the dorm complexes was the "Castle," the small grill that still exists in the basement of Bonnycastle dorm (the Glass Hat, the counterpart of the Castle for the Alderman

Road dorms, was then under construction). When my children were students at UVA decades later, I was amazed at how the dining opportunities in both choice and quality had increased exponentially—salad bars, sushi, paninis, ethnic foods, etc. These were as futuristic as PCs and cell phones in the 1960s.

Before departing the dining section of this tome, I would be remiss in not mentioning a particularly idiosyncratic venue that most Cavaliers of my era remember fondly. If one today ventures down into the bowels of Old Cabell Hall and enters the music department library, they will be treading in the footsteps of thousands of old Wahoos who sought refuge in the "Cave" for a cup of java and a glazed donut. The Cave was pretty much the only spot in the central classroom vicinity to get some refreshments and rest between classes. Back then, it was directly accessible from New Cabell Hall, where the great bulk of liberal arts courses were held. We all can remember the vaulted white ceilings (it had originally been a coal storage area), settling into those old comfortable leather couches with your jolt of caffeine and sugar, reading the *CD* or working on its crossword puzzle, and hopefully not falling asleep and missing your next class.

Back to pledging. In addition to meals, there were many pledge functions that brought one over to the house on a regular basis. Several of these functions provided manual labor for the brothers—for example, we acted as waiters for dinner, cleaned up the kitchen after the nightly "snacks" ritual (each weekday night, the kitchen was open at 11 p.m. to allow the brothers to sate their hunger built up by a tough evening of studying—or playing cards, or watching the tube, or whatever), and provided various painting and maintenance services.

As regards the latter, our house, although one of the less attractive ones at UVA, was in relatively good condition. It was a fairly new structure and, unlike the veritable "pigsties" that many of the fraternities at UVA have evolved into presently, it was very well maintained. The main reason for this was the work of our two "houseboys"—Jim Hicks and Jim Taylor. While the terminology is certainly not politically correct in modern society, that was the job description at the time. The two Jims cleaned the house on a daily basis, made the beds, served as bartenders at parties and were general go-to guys with any problems. Hicks in particular, who was the senior of the two, was a house fixture, was made an honorary brother, and could often be found regaling house members with tales of his various X-rated exploits. As was the case with meal service, I don't know when the fraternities stopped employing domestic staff on a regular basis, but the result has been many houses looking like a motorcycle gang had just visited for fun and games.

*AEPi house in 1966—one of the less aesthetically pleasing houses on Grounds*

Shortly after pledging began, we were assigned "big brothers," whose job was to provide "brotherly" guidance as we traveled on our journey to brotherhood. In my situation, the concept took on a new meaning. My big brother was Mike Schmerin, a second-year student from Johnstown, Pennsylvania. That selection was a life changer for me. Not only would Mike be a great big brother in the traditional fraternity sense, providing advice and guidance, he would become my lifelong friend, personal physician and a true "brother" in a real-life sense. We have had thousands of hours of adventures together. I was with him the moment he met his wife-to-be, and it was at his dinner table that it was suggested that I go out with my future bride. When asked about the benefits of the Greek system, I submit as Exhibit A my friendship with my "big brother."

And then there was the "hazing" aspect of pledging. I remember when my daughter pledged her sorority at UVA, I was amazed at the nature of her pledging experience—it was basically how many gifts and compliments that could be showered on her in a few short weeks. That was not the case for fraternities then or now. In recent years, fraternity hazing has become a national issue—and in many cases rightfully so. Putting someone's health at risk is never acceptable. But exactly what constitutes "hazing"? At UVA, hazing is now prohibited by University policy and is defined by the Office of the Dean of Students as any action "that is designed to or produces mental or physical harassment, discomfort or ridicule." A pretty broad definition without doubt. Seriously, if the University wants to do away with any action that produces mental discomfort, they should consider outlawing final exams; and as for ridicule, how about banning any grade less than a B. Ditto as to the training for any varsity sport. But, no matter how one defines "hazing," it was rampant by any standard at UVA's fraternities in the 1960s. However, it was something that was expected if not welcomed—one of the accepted practices of the era.

At the AEPi house, hazing took two basic forms—physical and psychological. The physical aspect was straightforward juvenile nonsense. Every few months, we were summoned to the house at night for a "shit session." The essence of this puerile activity was to gather us all in the party room, have us strip down to our underwear, and then proceed to douse us with every conceivable condiment and foodstuff from the kitchen (think ketchup, mustard, mayonnaise, eggs, etc.) while we were undertaking various calisthenics. This boorishness went on for about an hour, and then we were allowed to leave. Since the brothers did not want us to foul their washrooms, we were not allowed to shower at the house—thus, most of us did the mile trek back to the dorms in our underwear, holding our clothes in our arms so not to trash them with our assorted new body coatings. Those were childish antics, but it never really bothered me, and most of us just laughed at the absurdity of it all. Having said that, I remember that it once took me about a week of shampooing to get the smell of Worcestershire sauce out of my hair.

The psychological hazing was another thing altogether. This aspect of pledging mostly manifested itself in a series of "goat courts" (a "goat" being a derogatory term for a pledge). This was some nasty stuff and, as far as I was concerned, had no redeeming social value. The pledges were brought over to the house, stripped down, blindfolded and escorted into a series of rooms individually. After being told to lie on the floor facing up with your head resting on a cinderblock, the blindfold was removed. The room was dark except for a high-beam light shining directly in your face. There then followed a psychological browbeating that I assume was meant to extinguish any sense of superiority or cockiness. This Orwellian interrogation went on in several different rooms with a separate cast of interrogators in each room. While we weren't waterboarded, I'm not sure that what went on at Abu Ghraib was very much worse. Some of those brothers were pretty adept at psychological warfare. Later on, as a brother on the other side of the spotlight, I witnessed a 6'2", 230-pound football player brought to tears in less than two minutes. Fortunately, by my fourth year, this form of hazing had been eliminated. While the argument was made that shared adversity brings a group close together, a concept I was re-introduced to during basic training in the pre-volunteer army, I found nothing positive about this type of behavior. But as Joe E. Brown said in the final line of the classic movie Some Like It Hot, "Well, nobody's perfect."

And finally, there was the one-off "midnight goat walk." I remember this night every time I drive down a certain road in Charlottesville. One night not long after pledging began, we were all summoned to the house at about midnight, blindfolded, and each of us was tossed into the back of a waiting auto. I knew some others were in the auto with me, but did not know who or where we were going. After about half an hour of driving around, the car stopped and we were instructed to get out but not to take off our blindfolds until the car left.

As we heard our car and others pull away, we ripped off our blindfolds to find our whole pledge class stranded in the pitch black by a body of water. We soon started walking in the direction we had heard the departed cars going. It was a totally deserted area with the road bordered by empty pastures and wood railings, and none of us had any idea where we were. As we were walking, I found myself talking to different groups of guys, including some fellows whom I had not yet gotten to know very well. After about two hours (our journey was interrupted a few times due to one of the guys having an unfortunate bout of the runs), we finally hit Route 29 and figured out where we were. We had been dropped off at the reservoir on Hydraulic Road, which back then was totally barren territory. We were back in the dorms in another hour or so. While such action would never stand muster in today's culture—someone could have wandered off the unlit road and been gored by an errant bull—there actually was some method in that madness. The event brought many of us closer together and was a unifying factor for the group.

*The AEPi family in 1969*

All in all, it has to be said that, at least at the AEPi house, the brothers did something right. It is now the fiftieth anniversary of our pledging as I write this, and I would say that about half of the pledge class is still in regular communication with each other. At our forty-fifth UVA class reunion, seven AEPi's showed up out of a total of eighty-some-odd participants—the largest contingent from any organized group in our class. While my two closest friends in AEPi were in the class ahead and the class behind me, that group of twenty guys will forever be emblazoned in my mind—the brilliance of Margulies and Brener, the antics of Rubenstein, Blums, Reichard, Zippy, Shu, and the Big T, the all-around nice guy comfort of Shaky, Siegel, Levitt, Paley, Bear, and the Kid—the memories have not diminished much over the decades.

Say what you will about fraternities—and a lot of negative things have increasingly been said over the years—they create an atmosphere and culture that engenders personal and institutional loyalties. For example, after more than twenty-five years of assisting University Development in fundraising, I am aware that Greek members give at a materially higher rate than independents. Some claim that fraternities are elitist institutions. Some probably are, many are not—and in any event, they are probably not any more elitist than most self-chosen entities—say, for example, law firm partnerships or college faculties. Another criticism is that fraternities are limiting socially and intellectually. Again, some may be, but in my experience, most fraternities strongly encouraged involvement in other University activities and organizations. I know that I would not have met and interacted with nearly as many other UVA students if I had not been a fraternity member. And historically, the cumulative Greek GPA has exceeded the independent GPA more often than not.

At the end of the day, fraternities are no more than a bunch of people who choose to spend a lot of time together. In reality, they are no different from many ethnic, religious or cultural groups that choose to do the same. Most fraternity members are in search of a group that they can feel comfortable with. In a sense, fraternities are the original "safe spaces," a place where you can always comfortably retreat to, and thus a foundation that allows one to branch out and experiment with other activities and people—because you always know you can go home.

## The Halls of Academia

There actually were other activities going on at the University besides going down the road, big weekends, and rush. While Virginia did not have the academic standing in the 1960s that it now enjoys, it had a rigorous course of studies, and most Wahoos took their studies seriously. As noted earlier, classes were a six-day-a-week endeavor rather than the three- or four-day-a-week reality that now exists for many students. As is the case today, UVA had very strong departments in the humanities and social sciences, with particularly stellar faculties in English, history, and economics.

Having said that, I must admit that I did not find the overall academic atmosphere in Charlottesville to be quite as challenging as it had been in the highly competitive NYC high school milieu. At that time, UVA still had a significant number of prep school underachievers and an in-state contingent that was in no way as competitive as it is today. However, at the top of the class, we had as talented a group as at any premier college in the country. I believe one reason for that was that in 1966, regionalism was more important than it is presently, resulting in many top students from the South choosing to stay in the South rather than living amongst the Yankees. I knew a number of classmates who had turned down admissions to the Ivies in order to remain south of the Mason-Dixon Line. Indeed, there were many brilliant people in my class, including an individual who has been singled out more than once as one of the guiding lights of my generation. Francis Collins, from Staunton, Virginia, led the U.S. Genome Project, was the Director of the National Institute of Health and is a recipient of the Presidential Medal of Freedom. One would have to say that Francis came by this honestly, as I believe he was the only member of the class of 1970 to graduate with a 4.0 GPA.

Speaking of grades, the 1960s was a pre-grade-inflation era. We had not yet reached the situation where concern for students' self-worth and pressure from parents to get a bang for their tuition buck has led to grades lower than a B becoming almost as rare as a Republican on the faculty. Maintaining a B average was a tough task in those days, as witnessed by the fact that a 3.0 GPA was sufficient to make dean's list. And Intermediate Honors, which was awarded after second year to the top ten percent of the class, was defined by a 3.2 GPA. In contrast, by the mid-2010s, the average GPA for undergraduates was about a 3.3. The days of the "Gentleman's C" are far in the past.

There did exist a strange anomaly in calculating one's GPA at that time: all variations of a letter grade counted the same. Thus a B+, B and B- were of equal value in determining a GPA—leading to some obviously unfair results. For example, someone who had all A- grades would have a 4.0 GPA, while someone with all B+ grades would have a 3.0 average, which would be the same as a person with all B- grades. This never made any sense and was finally rectified during my fourth year.

One great attribute of UVA that I was able to take advantage of immediately was its long, honored tradition of having all professors, no matter how esteemed or famous, teach large groups of undergraduates. UVA has always been a teaching college. My first year, I was privileged to have Howard Hamilton teach biology and Robert Morgan teach American government. Both were full professors, superb lecturers and fully engaged with their students. I don't believe many institutions would have had as accomplished academicians as these teaching introductory courses. It was, and still is, a tribute to the faculty at UVA that so many professors remain committed to teaching and having personal contact with their undergraduate students.

~~~~~

Before I knew it, the time came to head home for Christmas break. As I noted earlier, in 1966 exams did not take place until after the holiday vacation. I took many of my school books back to NYC in anticipation of beginning the exam preparation process. However, my recollection is that I barely cracked a book once at home, spending most of my time catching up with my hometown buddies and regaling them with tales from UVA (remember there were no cell phones or email back then). Thus, it was with some trepidation that I returned to Charlottesville for my first bout with final exams.

I think most first-year college students are somewhat unsure whether they can compete on the college stage at the same level they did in high school. It was therefore with great relief that I emerged from first semester with four As and a B, thus putting to rest my parents' concerns that I had spent too much time rushing, pledging, and partying. I had assured them that a well-balanced student was more likely to be a happy student, and thus a successful one. All work and no play…

A new year (1967) and a new semester arrived. With the excitement of starting college, rush and finals behind me, I settled down to a relatively mundane routine dominated by classes and pledging. Overall for myself and the University, it was a fairly uneventful semester. Having said that, a few noteworthy incidents did take place that spring.

## *A Hint of Coeducation*

In April, the UVA Board of Visitors ("BOV") cracked open the door to the concept of coeducation at UVA. The BOV empowered President Shannon to conduct a study as to the "need" for coeducation—and if such "need" was found, a follow-up study on "feasibility" was mandated.

One would think that this was a relatively modest opening gambit on the subject of coeducation—a "need" study to be followed by a "feasibility" study—the types of things that bureaucrats do when they want to avoid doing anything. Nevertheless, the reaction to even this weak hint of coeducation was instant and harsh. *The Cavalier Daily* immediately noted the "violent student reaction against the suggestion" and promptly issued an editorial that was extraordinarily strident and hostile, even for that time period: "We want to stress from the outset of such debate that we look with horror upon the prospect of a large-scale female invasion, other than for the purposes of a party weekend, of these traditionally male Grounds." Now tell us how you really feel! Not much wiggle room for debate there. The *CD*'s point of view was seconded by Dean Runk in somewhat more measured tones as he was quoted as saying that he opposed such a move "lest the unique atmosphere of the University be lost."

In retrospect, the most interesting aspect of the reaction to the modest beginnings of a move toward coeducation was not the strong initial opposition, which was predictable given the mood of the time, but rather how quickly this antagonism would give way to a somewhat reluctant acceptance of reality and then outright approbation. The days of the "Gentleman's University" were now clearly numbered, and the *CD*'s editorial stance would seem a relic of the past within a remarkably short period of time.

## *"Hoot" Gibson Fires a Blank*

A few weeks after the brouhaha over the mention of coeducation, another contentious suggestion was made that raised the hackles of students and administrators alike. The UVA basketball coach, Bill "Hoot" Gibson,[30] shook everyone up by proposing that the basketball team all live together in the Alderman Road dorms and all eat together in Newcomb Hall. Again, a fairly modest proposal that today just seems part of the way things are. But that was not the case in 1967 Charlottesville, where the concept of real student-athletes was taken seriously as part of the Old U creed.

In actuality, Coach Gibson's suggestion was not surprising, representing as it did an attempt to inject some life in what was a moribund UVA basketball program. As of April 1967, the Wahoos had not had a winning season in thirteen years. Their record for the past eight seasons had been an astonishing 50-145. The previous season had been the first

---

30  For those under the age of sixty, "Hoot" Gibson was one of the first cowboy film actors.

since 1958 in which the team had won at least nine games. So, in his fourth year as coach, the "Hooter" was trying to stir things up. The football program quickly made a similar request. But, the Old U would have none of it.

In a very prescient editorial entitled "What Price Glory," *The Cavalier Daily* eviscerated Coach Gibson's attempt to segregate a group of athletes from their fellow students:

> What has happened to the concept of liberal education? Under the proposed system, athletes will come to the University, spend most of their time on the field, in the gym, or in the dorm, and will get to know their fellow teammates very well. But will they ever be exposed to a variety of viewpoints? Will they form any close friendships outside the narrow circle of the team? Will they become social beings? After four years what will they be prepared for? Playing pro ball?

As was the case with coeducation, the *CD*'s opposition was echoed by Dean Runk. He was quoted as asserting that athletic dorms were "foreign to the University" and that "the primary purpose in coming to the University is to be a University student and then an athlete, not an athlete and then a student." And, as was the reality at the time, Dean Runk had the final say. He determined that University housing would not be available for athletic teams as groups.

Interestingly, as was the case with coeducation, this initial virulent opposition would soon give way to an increasingly apparent reality. By 1968, the University approved scholarship athletes living together, as long as it was spread among multiple dorms—another example of 1966-1967 being the last gasp of the Old U.

As for the basketball team, they would not have a winning season while I was an undergraduate, and as we shall see, would soon experience a period of significant headline-producing turmoil. The program would finally turn around the year after I graduated with the appearance of Barry Parkhill—"Mr. BP"—who would subsequently lead the Cavaliers to their first 20-game victory season since 1928 and their first-ever post-season tournament appearance.

## The Charlottesville Bubble

During my first year, there was intermittent talk on Grounds of the "Charlottesville bubble," referring to a distinct insular culture thriving in Charlottesville that was pretty much oblivious to what was transpiring in the outside world. While UVA was no Shangri-La lost in the foothills of the Blue Ridge Mountains, there was much truth in the bubble notion. By 1966, the great social revolution of the 1960s was well underway in many parts of the country. The two leading edges of that phenomenon—the civil rights and anti-Vietnam War movements—were almost daily headlines in the media. Both were very much part of my high school experience in NYC. But in Charlottesville, you could barely notice that either existed.

This prevailing lack of interest in the travails of the real world was well recognized on Grounds, as illustrated in the following editorial comment in the *CD*: "There being no pressing issues concerning the University for us to rant about today, we have decided to alienate all those who abhor reading anything in *The Cavalier Daily* about the outside world, by jotting down a few inflammatory statements on that old bugaboo, Vietnam." Indeed, that old "bugaboo," the Vietnam War, had been escalating rapidly since the Gulf of Tonkin incident in August 1964. A major anti-war demonstration had taken place in Washington, D.C. in April 1965, and there was constant news of growing unrest on college campuses. But at UVA, there were no demonstrations and nary a peep of protest. While this would change dramatically in a few years, that was a world away, and during my first year all I can remember is one of the few lonely "radicals" walking around the dorms in his army fatigue jacket handing out anti-war leaflets and being roundly jeered and razzed.

And as for the civil rights movement, as noted earlier, Charlottesville and UVA were barely emerging from the days of massive resistance. With only a handful of black students, no black athletes and "Dixie" still being gloriously played at sporting events, civil rights as a movement was a non-sequitur at UVA. Nevertheless, some minor rumblings were beginning to be heard during spring semester, 1967. In March, the Student Council announced it would conduct a study of discrimination in fraternities, and toward the end of the semester, in May, the council took the position that all businesses pursuing a policy of discrimination should be off-limits for University organizations. *The Cavalier Daily's* reaction to the latter proposal was as swift and negative as its response to the possibility of coeducation. An editorial entitled "Council Oversteps Itself" stated, "We find such coercive action radically inconsistent with the tenets of freedom of choice and decision on which this institution was founded." Thus, the *CD*, as well as probably a majority on Grounds, were not yet ready to support even modest civil rights measures. However, as was the case with coeducation, this type of thinking would shortly be a thing of the past. It represented the last gasps of a sheltered, insular community that would soon be gone with the wind.

## *Wahoo Forever*

Before I knew it, spring semester classes were over and I entered exams with some trepidation, wondering if my first semester success was a fluke. Well, second semester turned out to be even better—I aced every course and thus ended my first year with about a 3.9 GPA. I mention this not to pat myself on the shoulder or to brag, but because it opened the door to possibilities I had not previously considered. Knowing that I had previously had my heart set on going to an Ivy League school, several of my friends and family members suggested that I consider transferring to an Ivy. They believed that I could probably get into the Ivy of my choice—an opportunity that had not existed for me coming out of high school—and given my GPA, they were probably right.

I recall considering the possibility for about five minutes. Yes, the prospects of being at Yale or Princeton were certainly enticing. But then I remembered what a wonderfully transformative year I had just experienced in Charlottesville. How much I had grown both socially and intellectually—the two being very much intertwined. How much I had broadened my horizons. I thought of the magnificent beauty of Mr. Jefferson's Grounds, of the distinctive values that were so idiosyncratic to UVA, of all my new buddies at AEPi and how much we had gone through together—and I knew that I would never leave Charlottesville and the U—I was now a Wahoo forever.

# —SECOND YEAR—
## Cracks in the Foundation
### *1967-1968*

# Introduction

I spent the summer of 1967 doing what I would do every summer as an undergraduate. I was a camp counselor at Camp Na-Sho-Pa in the Catskill Mountains. I had been introduced to this camp in 1965 by my closest childhood friend, Mike Shapiro, who also happened to be one of the top scholastic sprinters in NYC. I started there as a waiter and by 1967 was a full counselor. It was a time when summers were mostly spent making some money and not necessarily padding one's résumé, so a camp counselor's job was ideal. I spent most of the summer outdoors and doing physical activities, all expenses were covered and I made enough money from salary and tips to cover my out-of-pocket expenses for the following school year.

And, as it turned out, it was a perfect counterpoint to my life at UVA. The camp was very coed and very New York, and the adult population there embraced the "sex, drugs, and rock & roll" culture years before it would make an appearance in Charlottesville.

In any event, the summer of 1967 was the dawning of the Age of Aquarius for many of us. It was the summer of the Beatles' "Sgt. Pepper's Lonely Hearts Club Band," the Doors' "Light my Fire," Jimi Hendrix's "Are You Experienced," and Cream's "Disraeli Gears." It was subsequently deemed the "Summer of Love" by many in the media. The epicenter was San Francisco, where an estimated hundred thousand people converged on the Haight-Ashbury neighborhood for a summer of free love and psychedelic fantasy. While I can't say that my summer camp was a mini Haight-Ashbury, the atmosphere there certainly had more in common with San Francisco than with Charlottesville.

It was a great summer. I fell in love for the first time and, perhaps more importantly, solidified friendships with a group of a half-dozen guys who would be there with me every summer and who, in effect, constituted our own little fraternity in the Catskills. It was a hardscrabble bunch of guys, mostly from Queens, who had grown up playing slap ball, touch football, and stick ball in the streets or in the concrete public school playgrounds. Most probably hadn't worn a coat and tie since their bar mitzvahs. They were a crazy crew—Sucoff, Rauch, Sultan, Welsh, Lereah,[31] Cohen. Our shenanigans were legendary, and as was the case at UVA, much of our behavior wouldn't be tolerated in current society. But they were more forgiving times back then. For me, those friends were, and still are, highly entertaining and incredibly loyal, and during those summers they provided me with a much-needed emotional and mental release from the rigors of trying to be a serious scholar and student leader back at the University.

While I had a wonderful summer, by mid-August when camp ended, I was chomping at the bit to be back at UVA. I was able to spend a few weeks with my folks, who had not seen much of me over the past year, and then headed down to Charlottesville in my newly acquired road car—a used 1963 Chevy Nova convertible. I was due back at the AEPi house early to help clean up the house, give it a fresh coat of paint, participate in one last pledge trip and prepare for finally becoming a brother. So I moved into my room at the house with my closest pal in the pledge class, Dave Blumberg. A few days later, a letter came that would very much alter my course at Virginia.

## *Back to McCormick Road*

During the spring semester of my first year, I had submitted an application to be a first-year dormitory counselor for the following school year. I was interested in being a dorm counselor for several reasons. First, I enjoyed counseling and thought I was pretty good at it. Second, the job came with the perk of having your own free room. And third, I had heard that the counselor position was an important first step toward becoming active in student leadership on Grounds. Before the end of the semester, I received news that I had not been selected,

---

31 Mike Lereah would join me down at UVA in the fall of 1967 and pledge AEPi. So for the next three years, I would see him virtually every day, either in Charlottesville or at camp.

but had a high position on the alternate list. While I was somewhat disappointed, I was not surprised. Counselor selection was very much in the hands of the current counselor group, which in turn was pretty much dominated by a group of select fraternities, as was so much else at UVA at the time. Anyway, I was also looking forward to living in the fraternity house, so I was not too upset.

Well, what I didn't know was that I was actually number one on the counselor alternate list. So when one of the new counselors stepped down for personal reasons just as the new class of first-years was arriving, I was offered the position. Although I had already moved into the house, the AEPi brothers were very supportive of my taking the position (it was always beneficial for rush to have a brother in the dorms as a counselor). So I gathered my meager possessions and moved back to the familiar surroundings of the McCormick Road dorms.

Shortly after moving into 108 Metcalf and getting to know the incoming first-year students on the corridor, I had an opportunity to meet the counselor on the adjoining corridor, Steve Hayes. And this was the beginning of a lifelong friendship. Although Steve was also a second-year man, we had not met the previous year. Nonetheless, there was an immediate kinship between us—we were two public school kids from the New York City area (Steve had gone to high school in Smithtown, New York, in Suffolk County on Long Island). However, I soon learned that Steve was far more knowledgeable than I about the ins and outs of life at the University. This resulted from the fact that Steve's older brother, Ed, who was only a year ahead of us, had already established himself as a rising politico around Grounds, despite his strong New York accent and rough streetwise smarts.[32] Ed was a newly minted senior counselor in the dorms—which was the mark of a "made man" at UVA in those years. He had imparted to Steve an insider's knowledge of how things really worked at the University, and

---

32   Ed Hayes would go on to become a well-known prosecutor and celebrity lawyer in NYC. The character of Tommy Killian in Tom Wolfe's *Bonfire of the Vanities* is modeled after Ed, and the book is dedicated to him. Ed's autobiography, *Mouthpiece*, recounts some of his experiences at UVA.

over the following weeks, Steve would impart that knowledge to me. I learned how the established system operated, which fraternities controlled which areas of student life and what were the appropriate paths for achieving success as a student leader (becoming a dorm counselor being one).

It soon became clear to me that the power structure at UVA was a somewhat-gentrified version of Tammany Hall. The major elected positions on Grounds, such as Student Council, Judiciary Committee, and Honor Committee chair and vice-chair, had for years been controlled by the fraternities through their two political caucuses—Skull & Keys and Sceptre societies. Other major non-elective student organizations, such as the University Union and *The Cavalier Daily*, were also fraternity controlled; and because they were not subject to the general student electorate, they tended to be controlled by a select group of fraternities—sort of like the Roman patriarchy. It was a fascinating education, and I was an eager student.

In addition to the insider education I received, I very much enjoyed counseling the incoming class. I found it as rewarding as I had anticipated. It was also a very broadening experience. I not only got to meet many members of the class of 1971, I also got to know most of the other dorm counselors fairly well and thus wound up with friends in most of the other fraternity houses. It was clearly a great opportunity to branch out from the relatively contained group of students I had socialized with my first year. Perhaps even more importantly, Steve Hayes would become my closest friend and confidante in my class and would closely share with me the events of the next three years. After graduation and law school, we both wound up as young attorneys in NYC, where Steve would become one of the foremost entertainment lawyers in the country. Our friendship, forged in the halls of Metcalf House, would only become stronger as the years passed, and for forty years we had lunch together on a weekly basis until I decided to abandon NYC and return to the purple shadows of the Lawn.

## *Brotherhood*

While we had all just experienced the Summer of Love, love was not at the top of the list at the AEPi house as we gathered for "hell night."[33] I think pretty much every fraternity pledge back then somewhat feared the horrors awaiting them on hell night—the final step to brotherhood. One could only imagine the depravities lurking in the minds of some of the more deranged brothers. But, as it turned out, it was mostly an anti-climactic non-event. What we endured was basically an extended "shit session"—been there, done that. Frankly, most of the brothers did not seem to have their hearts in it and appeared to just be going through the motions.

While we seemed to get off relatively easily, this apparently was not the case for many of my friends in other houses. I heard stories of having to wear burlap underwear for a week, paddling and other demented physical abuse that would probably result today in suspension, expulsion or legal action. But that is now, and this was then—it was a different era—and everyone, students and administrators alike, took it in stride.

With brotherhood came responsibilities—the greatest one being preparing for and participating in rush. Rush, of course, is the lifeblood of the fraternity system, and the brotherhood took it very seriously. For AEPi back then, it was somewhat easier than for most of the houses because we had a limited pool of rushees—basically the Jewish first-year men. However, in 1967 this changed to a degree, as the brotherhood decided to consider a limited number of non-Jewish members for the first time. In any event, a rush list was prepared using the first-year face-book and word of mouth as its primary sources. Our original rush list for 1967 contained about a hundred names.[34] As rush unfolded, I was actually very impressed by the time, effort and diligence of the brothers coupled with a surprising fairness in the process.

---

33 While some fraternities had "hell week" as well—the AEPi's pretty much focused on the one night event.

34 A copy of the 1967 rush list resides in the Gardner Archives, as does the facebook.

The heart of the selection process was the weekly "ball session," which would week by week winnow down the names on the rush list. I know that each house had its own distinct set of rules and procedures—ours was quite transparent and relatively democratic. The days of passing around a box with different size and color balls in it so that one could vote anonymously were long gone at AEPi. At each session, every person on the list was discussed openly, followed by a full public vote of the brotherhood. It took three "black balls" to remove a person from consideration, and for each black ball there was an available "challenge," whereby a brother could speak in favor of the person. After each challenge, another vote would be taken. As you might imagine, with scores of candidates involved, each one of these sessions was lengthy and intense, often lasting into the early hours of the morning. It wasn't a perfect system, but it was about as open and fair a selection system as I've witnessed in a lifetime. It was also a process that clearly sharpened your advocacy and negotiating skills and gave one experience in the arts of social interaction and compromise. These were life lessons you didn't learn in the classroom.

The fruit of our labor was a new pledge class of about twenty guys, notable in that it included the first non-Jewish pledges in anyone's memory. While most of us didn't think it was as strong a class as the previous year, it did include a pledge destined to become one of the most outstanding leaders of the UVA Class of 1971—Steve Brickman, who would be presented with the coveted Algernon Sidney Sullivan Award for his class. Steve and I would spend the next three years and three more years in law school as great friends and colleagues, a relationship that has continued to the present. I feel it safe to say there was no more respected student at the University during that period than Steve—often referred to in law school as the "roving reasonable man." Things have not changed since that time, as Steve remains a class leader as an alum and a widely admired and honored member of the Birmingham community.

Having achieved brotherhood, and consequently having more free time without pledge duties, I decided to begin to branch out with my activities on Grounds.

## Expanding Horizons

I often tell students that I interact with that what you do outside the classroom is as important, or even more important, than what you do inside. The extracurricular activities one chooses to involve him or herself with can both broaden and enhance the college experience and allow one to develop social and leadership skills not available to those spending most of their hours outside of class in Alderman or Clark libraries. The key is the balance—and there are plenty of hours outside the lecture halls to both pursue course studies and participate in other meaningful activities.

My choices to expand my horizons were in the athletic and literary areas. I have always loved sports, and given my somewhat limited abilities, had participated in numerous athletic activities prior to college. However, I had clearly not achieved a level sufficient to be a college varsity athlete. Nevertheless, I was a willing sport, and my buddy Dave Blumberg convinced me to try out for UVA's rugby team. For those uninitiated in the joys of rugby, it is basically a mixture between British football (soccer) and American football, highlighted by the fact that it is a major contact sport with no padding or helmets. At UVA, as at most colleges, rugby was a club sport—meaning it was not supported financially by the University and was not under NCAA purview. However, it was well organized and had a full schedule of intercollegiate and club games. In fact, at that time, UVA probably had the best rugby team in the East and one of the best in the country. In the 1967-1968 season, the Wahoo ruggers had a 26-3-1 record.

In the fall of 1967, the club fielded three "sides" (teams)—denominated "A," "B" and "C" sides, with the A side being the best. Players at that time included undergraduates, graduate students and even some faculty. My friend Blums played on the A side, but I was neither big enough to play on the A-side scrum (equivalent to a football line) nor fast enough to be an A-side back. However, I was very pleased after weeks of practice to make the B-side scrum in the lock position. I played the full fall schedule and found the experience exhilarating. But my brief foray into intercollegiate sports came to a crashing halt in the spring season.

I had not been aware that varsity football players were allowed at that time to play spring rugby in order to stay in shape. I can still distinctly remember enduring that crushing tackle by a varsity safety or linebacker after having fielded a short kick during one of our inter-squad practices. It was the hardest hit I have ever experienced—and remember, ruggers don't wear any protective gear. As I barely limped off the field, with the bells still ringing, the thought came to me that it would be wise to be able to finish the semester in one piece. So, discretion being the better part of valor, I decided to forego the excitement of the game and the camaraderie so notably a part of that sport in order to ensure the future functionality of body and brain. And thus ended my collegiate sports career (other than IFC intramurals).

The literary part of my extracurricular endeavors was a more sedate affair. As previously noted, I had been a fairly successful high school journalist and thus decided to continue activities in this sphere. In 1967, there were four major student publications: *The Cavalier Daily*, the *Corks and Curls* yearbook, and two magazines—the *University of Virginia Magazine* (*UVM*) and the *Rapier*, a newly founded journal of "satire and broad discussion." Since several AEPi's were already active on the *UVM*, I decided to join that publication as my entry point into collegiate journalism.

The *UVM* had a long history at the University, having gone through various incarnations. By 1967, it was a mishmash of content and style. It contained articles that related to life on Grounds and national issues, and also included some attempts at poetry and creative writing. Taking up where I had left off in high school, where I had been a political and current events columnist, I focused on writing about the upcoming presidential election of 1968, which was already extraordinarily contentious and which would turn out to be one of the watershed events of the second half of the twentieth century. By spring semester, I had been named political editor of the magazine. My favorite article was one I penned about the emergence of Ronald Reagan on the national scene as a potential presidential candidate in 1968. The conventional wisdom was that he was too conservative and too much of a lightweight to ever be elected president. Having listened to his speech at the 1964 Republican Convention and followed his 1966 gubernatorial success in California, I thought otherwise, and predicted that he might well achieve the oval office in the future. As history unfolded, it was a prescient article, although it did take Dick Nixon's Watergate fiasco and Jimmy Carter's failed presidency to lay the groundwork for "The Gipper."

Notwithstanding my achievements at the *UVM*, I found the five-issue-a-year magazine format very limiting and was eager to set pen to paper more often. The *UVM* experience was quite positive in that it got my journalistic juices flowing again, and by third year, my efforts had shifted to *The Cavalier Daily*.

## They Paved Paradise and Put Up a Parking Lot [35]

Any person who has had the fortune of attending a concert in McIntire Amphitheatre[36] on a beautiful starlit evening or who has just sat on a bench in the amphitheatre on a spring afternoon with a book and a sandwich will probably be astounded to learn of the decision by the University administration that was projected into my consciousness when I unfolded *The Cavalier Daily* on September 28, 1967, while downing a doughnut and cup of java in the Cave. The entire right side

---

35  With compliments to Joni Mitchell and "Big Yellow Taxi."

36  McIntire Amphitheatre is a Greek-style outdoor theater located just west of the lower end of the Lawn behind Cocke Hall. It was only the seventh Greek-style outdoor theater in the nation when it was built in 1921 based on a gift from Paul McIntire, who also provided the funds to establish the McIntire School of Commerce and the McIntire School of Music at UVA.

of the *CD* was composed of a faux photograph of the Lawn divided into parking spaces with the headline: "Today the Amphitheatre, Tomorrow the Lawn." Until that point I, and I think most of my fellow students, were unaware that the powers-that-be at the U had decided in their infinite wisdom to extend the parking lot behind the amphitheatre[37] to the grass infield fronting the stage of McIntire. While there was a clear need for additional parking at the University, the very concept of turning the verdant beauty of the amphitheatre into a paved parking lot was astonishing. The fact that the administrators were actually doing it was horrifying. It took a few years, but by the early 1970s, McIntire was indeed an auto depository.

In retrospect, this decision can be viewed as part of a trend in the 1960s and 1970s to demolish historical structures in the name of progress. One of the most glaring examples of this in my hometown of NYC was the destruction of Stanford White's[38] magnificent Penn Station to make way for the monstrosity of the new Madison Square Garden. But unlike many other examples of paving over historical structures, the McIntire Amphitheatre story would have a happy ending—and I am proud to say that I had a role in that. Shortly after returning to the University for law school after my active-duty stint in the Army, I was elected to the Student Council. One of the first things I did in that capacity was to pen a resolution to petition the administration to return McIntire to its "verdant splendor." The resolution received unanimous support. By the spring of 1973, the faculty joined the students in vocally protesting in favor of regrassing the amphitheatre, and on May 1, 1973, more than two hundred students and faculty turned out to demonstrate for McIntire's restoration. An art professor was quoted as saying: "It's shocking to see cars in the amphitheatre—it's like taking a Gothic church and turning it into a brothel." Given the overwhelming support of the University community, the decision was

---

37  Bryan Hall did not exist at that time.

38  Stanford White also happened to be the architect of the post-fire renovated Rotunda and Old Cabell, Cocke and Rouss halls.

made shortly thereafter to reverse this aesthetic evil, thus leaving future generations of Wahoos with the lovely vision that exists today.

*What were they thinking?*

## In the Classroom with Two Giants

Little did I know in September 1967, when I sat down in Old Cabell Hall auditorium for my initial lecture in Economics 1, that I would be present at the first class taught at UVA by a young assistant professor who would go on to teach more than forty thousand Wahoos and become a legend on Grounds. Ken Elzinga had just arrived in

Charlottesville after receiving his Ph.D. at Michigan State. While barely having exceeded his twenty-fifth birthday, his relative youth did not preclude him from becoming an instant celebrity with the student body. I can remember him being invited to dinner at the AEPi house multiple times while I was there, an "honor" reserved for very few. He always attended and was always a big hit.

Needless to say, ECON 1-2 were two of my favorite classes at UVA. Mr. Elzinga was a superb communicator from day one, making you feel as if he was speaking directly to you even though you were in a large lecture hall with hundreds of other students. Perhaps this is why for many years, his lectures were the most attended on Grounds.

But, I believe it is far more than just Mr. Elzinga's teaching style that has endeared him to Wahoos for decades. I think we all realized that he was genuinely interested in his students as individuals. As the years passed and Mr. Elzinga became a renowned economist, consultant and author, his dedication to his students never waned. Recently, during the dark days of the Rolling Stone debacle,[39] Mr. Elzinga once again demonstrated his commitment to both the students at the University and the Jeffersonian ideal of following the truth wherever it may lead, when, to my knowledge, he became the only UVA professor or administrator to forthrightly and in writing apologize to the Phi Kappa Psi fraternity house for the opprobrium and abuse that was so unjustly heaped on them by various members of the University community. He has always been respected as a teacher in more than name only, as a person of true integrity and honor, and as a member of the UVA community who epitomizes the social compact between faculty and students that makes Virginia such a special place.

---

39    In November 2014, *Rolling Stone* magazine published an article entitled "A Rape on Campus," which detailed an alleged rape at the Phi Kappa Psi fraternity house at UVA. Before any investigation took place or any facts emerged, demonstrations were launched against the Phi Psi's, their house itself was physically desecrated and its residents forced to move out. A later investigation by the Charlottesville Police Department revealed no substantive basis to confirm the allegations, and an independent review by the Columbia School of Journalism found serious failures in journalistic standards by the magazine. *Rolling Stone* later retracted the article.

*Mr. Elzinga enjoying dinner at the AEPi house*

The other legend I had the fortune to study under in 1967 was already a well-established celebrity at UVA. Ray Bice (*see photo pg 40*) had been at Virginia for nineteen years when I plunked myself down in Gilmer Hall for his Psychology 1 course. Mr. Bice arrived in Charlottesville in 1948 after receiving his bachelors, masters and doctorate degrees at the University of Wisconsin, and was quoted as saying, "Once I saw the Grounds, it was love at first sight." It didn't take long for Mr. Bice to demonstrate his love for the University. In addition to becoming a popular psychology teacher, he was an administrative jack-of-all-trades at UVA, becoming an associate dean in the College of Arts & Sciences, assistant to the president, secretary to the rector and Board of Visitors, and the University history officer.

Most students first encountered Mr. Bice either by living in Kent or Dabney dorms, where he was the associated dean, or like myself, by taking his Introduction to Psychology course, affectionately known as "Bice Psych." His class was most famous for his "Bice Devices," a series of contraptions formed from a conglomeration of household items that he used to illustrate many of the more difficult concepts of psychology. He was an extraordinary man, beloved by his students, and was the recipient of the highest awards at the University, including the Thomas Jefferson Award and the Algernon Sydney Sullivan Award. As was the case with Mr. Elzinga, we knew he had a real interest in teaching and mentoring undergraduate students—an attribute that I would find unusually widespread among UVA professors, and something that truly distinguishes UVA from many of its peer institutions.

Mr. Bice did not retire from his duties at UVA until 1998 at the age of eighty. He passed away in 2012—truly a "UVA Great."

~~~~~

I would be remiss if I didn't mention that it was during second-year that I took the most useful and enduring academic course of my undergraduate career – History of Art from 1400 to the Present. I remember well sitting in Cocke Hall as various great works of art were projected onto the front screen and learning the back stories, trends, and nuances attendant to each piece. Henceforth, I was able to walk into virtually any great art museum in the world and at least have a basic appreciation of what I was viewing.

## The Bubble Deflates

As I settled into my second-year routine, I could sense a change in the atmosphere on Grounds. The Charlottesville bubble seemed to be slowly deflating. The vagaries of the real world were at the doorstep. The leading cause of the slow leak was the ever-present Vietnam War. There was no escaping the increasing realization that this conflict was very much becoming part of our lives. In reality, there was no place to hide. Not only was the war the preeminent news story of the day, but it was also about to intrude in our personal lives in a meaningful way.

By 1967, the war was rapidly escalating. The number of U.S. troops in Vietnam had more than doubled in the past two years, increasing from about two hundred thousand in 1965 to approximately five hundred thousand in 1967. And it appeared as if there was no end in sight—either to the troop increases or to the war itself. Any discerning person, even in the Charlottesville cocoon, could figure out that sooner rather than later the U.S. military would have to implement a broader-based draft. While we all had student deferments, rumors were already rampant that graduate school deferments were on the chopping block—and indeed in February 1968, draft deferments for most male graduate school students were abolished. This certainly brought the war home in a manner many of us could relate to.

Suddenly *The Cavalier Daily* was full of articles, editorials, and op-eds dealing with the war, and the first real anti-war activities became noticeable on Grounds. The *CD* set the tone with an early October editorial entitled "The Vietnam Tragedy" that condemned the war as an "abomination" that the U.S. "cannot win in an acceptable sense," and as an "inglorious struggle." A few weeks later, anti-war forces organized two buses to journey to Washington to participate in a national anti-war protest march on the Pentagon. In a first, a group of fifteen faculty members issued an open letter to the University community supporting the protest march and asserting the Vietnam conflict to be an "immoral and unjust" war.

However, the increase in anti-war rhetoric at UVA in the fall of 1967 was by no means indicative of a tidal wave of protest in Charlottesville. The University was still essentially a traditionalist bastion. Thus, while the Southern Student Organizing Committee (SSOC) was making plans for the buses to travel to D.C. for the protests, students were opposing the selling of tickets to the march in the student union; and while fifteen professors were openly opposing the war, a group of sixteen professors quickly retaliated by publishing a letter in opposition to the anti-war marches, claiming that Hanoi was as responsible for the war as the U.S. In a student poll held in the fall of 1967 in anticipation of the 1968 elections, every potential Republican candidate defeated every potential Democrat candidate.

So it was not as if UVA was suddenly becoming the Berkeley of the South. The real power of the anti-war movement would not be felt on Grounds for another two years. However, just as the Vietnam War had started to chip away at the foundations of "Eisenhower" and "Mad Men" America on a national basis, it had also begun to crack the foundations of the Old U and its ossified complacency. And along with this increasing anti-war restlessness came a growing focus on the other significant bubble deflator of the late 1960s—the civil rights movement.

I have already noted that during my first year, there was little discussion of civil rights, or the lack thereof, at the University or in its Charlottesville surroundings. This too began to change—particularly as the election year of 1968 dawned. It seemed as if suddenly someone had thrown on a switch, and the University's sad history of race relations was now out of the shadows. Just prior to first-semester exams, *The Cavalier Daily* published an editorial entitled "Slaves at the University," thus broaching a topic that had not often been the subject of polite conversation at UVA. In February 1968, the NAACP issued a protest against discrimination in the recruitment of black athletes at the University. A week later, a petition signed by over one thousand students, accompanied by a letter signed by faculty members, called for the University to apply a real integration policy—including making a sincere effort to recruit black students and faculty, taking actions to obtain non-discriminatory pledges from local landlords and adopting a strong rule prohibiting University organizations from using segregated facilities. At this time, there were only seventy-one black students enrolled at UVA out of a total of eighty-five hundred, and one black faculty member.

This sudden focus on the obvious racial issues extant at UVA actually led to some initial University actions to confront the inequities of its past and present. Shortly after the presentation of the student petition, Student Council passed an anti-segregation proposal in front of a packed house at Old Cabell Hall. Subsequently in April, UVA's comptroller set forth University policy on the use of segregated facilities, making it clear that "all official University groups refrain from using facilities which practice discrimination."

And finally, in May, the University clarified its policies regarding non-discrimination after a series of correspondence between President Shannon and the president of the local chapter of the Council on Human Rights. President Shannon, in addition to reasserting UVA's policy against using segregated facilities, listed a number of other steps being taken, including instituting a nondiscriminatory resale pledge for faculty mortgages and requesting the Student Council and University Union to cooperate in providing a non-discriminatory date housing list.

While these were certainly only baby steps, they were significant for the time and place. And in the following school year, civil rights issues would eclipse the anti-war movement as the focal point of student unrest. But in the spring of 1968, the foundations of the Old U were still basically intact, if showing signs of stress fractures. Even the horror of Martin Luther King's assassination in April did not bring about any particular acceleration of the bubble deflation. Classes were made optional the day of MLK's funeral and President Shannon eulogized him. However, in the wake of the ceremonies, things continued pretty much as usual.

Although the bubble was not yet ready to burst, there clearly was a recognition on Grounds that things were in flux and that the old order was slowly but surely giving way to a new set of priorities. This feeling was vividly expressed in the editorial introduction to the 1968 edition of the *Corks and Curls* yearbook, which noted that the typical Virginia man "once known chiefly for his legendary abilities at drinking Jack Daniels, rolling to Sweet Briar or Hollins, and choosing the 'gut' courses that guaranteed him his 'gentleman's C'" was giving way to a student that "spends much more time with his books" and that has a "healthy skepticism, an unwillingness to accept as sacred anything simply hallowed by age, an impatience with the paternalism of [his] elders." Thus, "In quiet, subtle ways the old institutions are being challenged." Well, beginning the following year, the challenges would neither be so "quiet" nor "subtle."

## *"Shitty" Is Dead*

Many college graduates, particularly after the passage of decades, remember few specifics of their time in the hallowed halls of academia. There are a number, such as myself, where the images of college days are still so vivid that they shine brighter than those of events of a few months prior. Yet of all those images, one that is among the strongest occurred on the morning of Thursday, March 21, 1968.

I woke up that morning in 108 Metcalf, put on my coat and tie, and headed to my first class of the day, which was Ray Bice's Psych 2 lecture course just across McCormick Road in Gilmer Hall. As usual, I walked into the lecture hall and joined a group of about a half dozen AEPi's who were also in the class and always sat together. One of the guys turned to me and asked whether I had heard what happened last night—knowing that (in a pre-cell phone, pre-internet era) I was probably out of touch with nightly events at the house. When I answered in the negative, he told me that, in anticipation of spring break, a bunch of the brothers had been up all night partying and carrying on—and that subsequently a few had gotten into a bad car accident on 14th Street on the way home. And then, in a flat matter-of-fact tone he said, "And Shitty is dead." ("Shitty" was the moniker of a boisterous, social, well-liked third-year brother in the house, who had garnered his nickname after having had an unexpected bodily malfunction during a party his first year.) I was totally stunned. Shitty was one of the first brothers at AEPi whom I had met during rush, and this was the first contemporary that I knew who had been so peremptorily removed from the world. Such things were not supposed to happen—although in actuality, I shouldn't have been surprised. Fatal car accidents were not such rare occurrences at UVA at that time. In fact, three Wahoos had been killed the previous semester on the way back to the U from a road trip to Sweet Briar. But I didn't know those guys, and Shitty was my friend.

In retrospect, the most amazing thing about the incident was how quickly it was forgotten. No lessons were learned. We all left for spring break, and shortly after returning it was Easters Weekend. There was no decrease in the amount of alcohol consumed or the number of guys getting into their cars after a party not capable of differentiating a stop-light from a strobe light or the road from the sidewalk. The exuberance and resilience of youth was quickly able to compartmentalize the incident and consign it to the distant past as if it never occurred. The best I can say is not that there were no further fatalities while I was at UVA, but only that I didn't know any of them.

## *The Fraternities Falter*

As noted earlier, the fraternities pretty much dominated all leadership aspects of undergraduate student life in the world of the Old U. This was somewhat amazing since fraternity members comprised less than half of the undergraduate student body. I guess there were several reasons for this. Maybe it was because the fraternities were more organized than the independents; maybe it was because that, in the Charlottesville bubble, no one got too excited about anything anyway; and maybe it was because that's the way it always had been—which was as good a reason as any at UVA in the mid 1960s.

But as UVA began to awaken from its decades-old torpor in the late 1960s, the old order of things began to crumble. This was initially evident in Student Council elections. Student Council was, and is presently, the University-wide body of student representatives that act in the name of the student body. In the late 1960s, the council had twenty-two members, nine of whom were from the College of Arts & Sciences. Traditionally, virtually all College members were fraternity men. And these members were selected in elections held twice a year, in the late fall and spring semesters. Most of the candidates running for council had previously been nominated by the two fraternity-dominated caucuses mentioned earlier—the Sceptre and Skull & Keys societies. These two societies had origins as student political parties dating back to the 1920s. By the 1950s, they had developed into fraternity-led caucuses with the essential purpose of nominating students for Student

Council, the Judiciary Committee and College officers (the heads of the Honor Committee).

The caucuses were like mini-conventions. Each fraternity had eight votes at the caucus. And, as is the case with many political conventions, most of the politicking and decision-making took place prior to the formal caucus itself. Since not much went on in terms of actual issues during the bubble era, the process of choosing candidates was very much personality driven. Each fraternity tended to have a few known "politicos," who would lead the house delegations at the caucuses. Getting the support of these politicos prior to the caucus was key to securing a nomination. As for the two caucuses, there were no ideological or other differences between them—Sceptre and Skull & Keys were Tweedledee and Tweedledum. While independents were nominally able to attend the caucuses, very few did. They were clearly creatures of the fraternities.

The worm had begun to turn for the fraternities in April 1967 with the creation of the University Party (the "UP"), a new independent-dominated student political group. In the spring 1967 Student Council elections, a UP candidate, Jacques Jones, was swept into office, receiving two hundred more votes than the closest other candidate. Jones had joined the UP after failing to secure a nomination from the Sceptre Society caucus. But this was still the Old U, and the other four College candidates elected were fraternity men. That election, however, was the veritable canary in the coal mine and was the last council election to be dominated by the fraternity caucuses.

The fall 1967 council elections would clearly demonstrate the vulnerability of the old order. That December, the two UP candidates, Pieter Schenkkan and Gordon Calvert, received the most votes of any of the candidates running. *The Cavalier Daily* noted, "There has been greater excitement about this election and more debate than in any in our near memory" and that there was "an increased interest in ideas." So suddenly ideas were "in," and the fraternity inspired "cult of personality" was rapidly losing favor.

But it was the council election in the spring of 1968 that was the coup de grace for the fraternity domination of Student Council. May arrived, the caucuses nominated their candidates, the UP nominated its candidates, and then out of the proverbial woodwork came Walker Chandler, Charles Murdock and the Anarchist Party—and everything changed. At first, the Anarchist candidacy seemed to be a "high camp" parody of the traditional UVA council elections. Their campaign poster was a humorous lampoon of the standard caucus poster—photos of a bomb-tossing Chandler and a grenade-toting Murdock accompanied by the slogans "Vote Anarchist—What Has Order Gotten You" and Chairman Mao's iconic slogan, "Political power grows out of the barrel of a gun."

Well, I don't believe the Grounds had ever witnessed anything quite like this. The Anarchists certainly shook up the established order and generated a level of interest in council elections that had not been witnessed in recent history. The result was the largest turnout the College had seen in years—sixty-three percent of those eligible to vote. Chandler and Murdock were swept into office, along with one UP candidate and two caucus candidates. Chandler received the largest number of votes a candidate for Student Council had ever received. For the first time in a generation, caucus candidates were less than half of those elected. Never again would the fraternity caucuses achieve a majority of the College candidates elected, and as we shall see, before the end of 1969, the decades-old caucuses would face oblivion.

And, as it turned out, the newly elected Anarchists were anything but parodies. They had very different personalities—Chandler was the outspoken, gregarious showman and Murdock the quiet, brooding intellectual. But both were serious radical reformers in that still-traditional UVA milieu, and although both would play roles in the significant changes that would occur the next academic year, they would not be its leaders.

So, by the end of my second year, the fraternities had lost their traditional power base in Student Council. But they still controlled the other undergraduate segments of student government—the Honor and Judiciary committees. Thus, while the student body was moving toward idea-oriented change in the political arena, it was still willing to back the old guard in the context of honor and social behavior. The reformist challenge to the Honor Committee was still a year away.

# VOTE ANARCHIST

*What Has Order Gotten You?*

Walker Lawrence Chandler

Charles Andrew Murdock

Political power grows out of the barrel of a gun.
- Chairman Mao

# STUDENT COUNCIL ELECTION
## Vote May 8-9   9 A.M. - 2 P.M.

*The Anarchists arise*

In one of those fascinating historical coincidences, on the same day that *The Cavalier Daily* announced the overwhelming Anarchist victory, it also announced that D. Alan Williams had been appointed Dean of Student Affairs, replacing Dean Runk, who would be stepping down as of June 30.[40] So the Anarchists were in and Dean Runk was out—truly the end of one era and the beginning of a new one.

~~~~~

After the brief flurry of excitement provided by the Anarchist campaign, life on Grounds quieted down in preparation for exams. I finished my last exam on June 3, packed up and headed home the next day. You may wonder how I remember the exact date I finished exams almost five decades ago. Well, it was because the events of the next few days left an indelible mark in my memory and the history of our country.

I arrived home for a late dinner on Tuesday, June 4. After dinner and downloading events of the past few weeks with my parents, I turned on the TV to watch the results of the crucial California Democratic primary. It was a key match-up between Eugene McCarthy and the recently surging candidacy of Robert Kennedy. President Johnson had previously shocked the nation with his announcement on March 31 that he would not seek reelection. The increasingly virulent anti-war movement, the challenges by McCarthy and then Kennedy and Johnson's failing health had driven him out of the race. McCarthy and Kennedy were fighting for supremacy of the left wing of the party and the right to take on Vice President Hubert Humphrey, who had announced his candidacy after Johnson's announcement and was sitting out the primaries. Whoever won the California primary would probably be Humphrey's main competitor at the convention in Chicago.

I stayed up past midnight to watch the results of the primary and went to bed only after watching Senator Kennedy make his victory speech, turning out the light after hearing his famous closing, "Now

---

40  Dean Runk's title of "Dean of the University" was to be discontinued—it exited with the man.

it's on to Chicago, and let's win there." Way too early the following morning, I heard a lot of noise outside my bedroom door. My father left for work before 7 a.m. every morning, but was generally very quiet in an effort not to awaken the rest of the household. My door suddenly opened and I saw my father standing there with a very troubled look on his face—not the usual visage that would be greeting his son just home from months away at college. The words "Bobby Kennedy was shot last night" still ring in my ears. I couldn't believe what I was hearing. It was staggering. Hell, it had been less than five years before when my tenth-grade history exam had been interrupted with the announcement over the PA system that President Kennedy had been shot. And Martin Luther King Jr. had been killed only two months ago. Three of the most famous men in our country assassinated in such a brief span of time—an unprecedented occurrence in our history. These were dark days, and the waves of tumult and change battering our nation were ready to descend on what was left of the bubble in Charlottesville.

# —THIRD YEAR—
## THE BUBBLE BURSTS
### *1967-1968*

# Introduction

If the summer of 1967 came to be known as the Summer of Love, then the summer of 1968 could appropriately be titled the "Summer of Turmoil." The scores of race riots across America following the murder of Martin Luther King Jr., the assassination of Bobby Kennedy, and the growing anti-war ferment flowing from the early 1968 Tet offensive in Vietnam[41] all set the stage for a summer of turbulence and heightened tensions that would culminate in the disastrous Democratic National Convention in August. That convention, held in a Chicago just recovering from major rioting in April, was disrupted by the activities of thousands of protesters, which in turn was met by a strong response from the Chicago police. The images of police in full riot gear battling with protesters were splashed across America's newspapers and TV news reports. It was not pretty, and it caused tremendous consternation throughout the nation.

While most of this was going on, I was ensconced once again in my other "bubble" community—that of Camp Na-Sho-Pa in the Catskills. Without the existence of PCs or cell phones, and with few TVs present, our camp existed in its own little universe for eight weeks. And what a fun world it was—outdoors most of the day participating in athletic activities and even some nights with a blanket on the baseball fields. There was a tremendous sense of camaraderie amongst my group of friends, and the real world was miles away. But all good things must

---

41 The Tet offensive was a series of surprise attacks launched by the North Vietnamese and Viet Cong in late January 1968 around the time of the Vietnamese New Year (Tet) celebrations. These attacks were initially successful, but the U.S. and South Vietnamese forces quickly counterattacked and inflicted heavy losses on the attackers. While the campaign was a military victory for the U.S. and its allies, it was a political defeat. Having been advised by the government that the war was going well, many in the U.S. were surprised by the strength of the coordinated offensive, and this led to a weakening of domestic support for the war.

come to an end (at least until the next summer), and as exceptional as things were at camp, I was even more excited about being back at UVA for my third year.

## *Change Is in the Air*

I arrived back in Cville early, as once again I was a counselor in the McCormick Road dorms—this time on first-floor Kent. I had a great group of first-years on my corridor and very much looked forward to the new academic year unfolding. But one thing was sure from the get-go—the tumultuous events of the summer had changed many attitudes around Grounds.

*In my Kent House dorm room 1968*

As an amateur historian, I recognize the difference between writing history from personal experience and writing history from contemporary documents. This endeavor is a combination of the two, and it is important to differentiate between the two as much as is possible. As strong as my memories of this period are, by necessity I have read every issue of *The Cavalier Daily* for this four-year period, if for no other reason than to refresh my recollections of events that transpired almost fifty years ago. In so doing, it is fascinating to observe what the advantage of time, historical context and life experience can add to a straightforward reading of contemporary documents. In retrospect, a reading of the *CD*'s editorial written over the summer (but before the Democratic Convention) for the 1968 orientation issue and a *CD* editorial written a few weeks later when classes began reflect a marked change in attitude by the University's leading journalists in a very short period of time. While the *CD*'s editorials by no means necessarily reflected the collective attitudes of the student body, they were an important barometer of current thought. In addition, in those pre-internet days, the *CD* was a more important source of information for the University community and was almost certainly more widely read than it is today. Most students picked up a copy daily on their way to class, if for no other reason than to find out how our sports teams had fared or to do the crossword puzzle while sitting in the back row of one's least favorite lecture class.

Responding to the shifting sands beginning to occur in the previous academic year, the *CD* editors had this to say to the incoming class in the Summer of 1968 orientation issue:

> Never before in its history has the University and everything for which it has always stood undergone the scrutiny it undergoes today. The students and administrators of Mr. Jefferson's institution are finally waking up to the fact that the University must keep up with the world around it; those who would defend the old concept of the University of Virginia are finally waking up to the fact that this concept and all aspects of it are no stronger than their ability to withstand challenge and change.

Of course, the University does not have a corner on the market of change. Everyone knows that what is going on here is going on everywhere to varying degrees. The all-important difference, however, is that here it is able to go on within a framework of gentlemanliness and honor. We would betray our founder if we allowed the pursuit of truth ever to be a cause of the type of activity which has occurred at some other institutions. Change and gentlemanliness are not irreconcilable.

So in effect, this was the message to the incoming Class of 1972: Welcome to this tradition-bound institution—but be forewarned, change is coming—but then again, it will come in an orderly and gentlemanly fashion. Very UVA indeed! However, this was written prior to the Democratic Convention in late August, and the *CD's* editorial that greeted all students on the first day of class on September 3 had a materially different tone, warning of a growing discontent that could manifest itself in unexpected ways:

> Phenomena like the Democratic Convention were the last straw for many concerned but not yet inflamed students. Students everywhere, even at the University of Virginia, are slowly or rapidly getting more and more fed up with the antics of a generation which seems determined in its attempt to doom us all to death in an unpopular, unwanted, undeclared war. We have seen demonstrations here, but no one has ever taken them very seriously except those who were in them. This year we will see more and more coats and ties among those demonstrators. Public expression of the growing discontent will no longer be reserved to those variously labeled "troublemakers," "weirdos," "beatniks," "hippies," etc. Nothing much has changed on the surface, but all  important changes have occurred underneath.

Look out, because when those changes manifest themselves on the surface, anything could happen.

So, we had progressed from gentlemanly change to anything could
happen. Well, in one sense, more prophetic words have rarely been
written. Within six months, activist demonstrations would be taking
place on Grounds in a manner never before seen in Charlottesville.
But interestingly, the stimulus for those demonstrations would not be
the Vietnam War, which was the tinderbox that ignited the flames at
the Democratic Convention. In fact, amazingly little would be heard
about the war on Grounds in the 1968-1969 academic year. Rather,
the cause of the disturbances to come would be the unfinished business
of the civil rights movement—which would finally come to fruition at
Mr. Jefferson's University in the spring of 1969.

As for myself, I was one of those who returned to Charlottesville
and noticed some of these changes, but didn't think too much would
come of it. Sure, there were a few less coats and ties around and hair
and sideburns were a bit longer; and sure, the Anarchists had shaken
things up a bit in the spring; and sure, the *CD* was ranting and rav-
ing as had become its wont; but all in all, the U seemed to be pretty
much the same place. And, indeed, things were pretty quiet for the
first few weeks of the semester. None of the turbulence flowing from
the Democratic Convention that was already evident on many college
campuses could be found on the Grounds.

The big news that marked the beginning of the school year, much
to the joy of many Wahoos of every political stripe, was the abrupt
death of the approved housing scheme. Interestingly, approved housing succumbed not to the growing trend of student control over their
personal lives or to the recognition that UVA would probably soon
be a coed institution, but rather to an attempt to begin making civil
rights reform a reality. The student-run University Union, which was in
charge of maintaining the approved housing listings in Charlottesville,
had sent out a hundred letters during the summer to approved housing candidates that contained for the first time a non-discrimination

pledge. Of the hundred who received the letters, only ten returned signed pledges—thus both demonstrating the still-widespread discriminatory ethos in Charlottesville and also de facto ending a viable approved housing network. Indeed, a week later, Hollins and Sweet Briar threw in the towel and, to the delight of all involved, announced that their students could stay in hotels and motels.

The other major piece of news that greeted us early in the semester was the announcement of UVA's first major capital expansion plan in decades. The University's physical development over the next thirty to forty years was essentially outlined in this announcement. Included in the plan was a significant expansion of building in the McCormick Road/Emmet Street sector that would include new science and engineering buildings and a new school of education; a fine arts center on Carr's Hill, including a new school of architecture; an expansion of the medical center, including a new school of nursing; and perhaps most significantly, the transposition of the law and graduate business schools away from central Grounds to a new "campus" to be known as the North Grounds. This would mark the first time that a material part of the student body would be attending classes away from Mr. Jefferson's Academical Village. While these plans would only come to fruition years in the future and affect very few students then walking the Grounds, it was very much a recognition that with coeducation on the horizon and given the constant pressure from the state legislature to admit more in-state students, the small, cozy nature of life at the University was about to become a thing of the past.

So while the seeds of change were in the air, it certainly appeared in the fall of 1968 that such change would come gradually. All in all, the bubble, though deflated, was still intact and much of the Old U was evident—as one can ascertain from the front-page lead article in the October 1 issue of *The Cavalier Daily* discussing the approaching Homecomings festivities: "Good conditions are also reported at the three Charlottesville ABC stores which guarantee an adequate supply of liquor for the weekend. The Barracks Road store, however, reports that it is out of Virginia Gentleman Bourbon." Out of Virginia Gentlemen, were they? A minor tragedy.

The student body as a whole had clearly not been radicalized by the summer events. A mock poll of the students in anticipation of the 1968 presidential election showed Richard Nixon narrowly defeating Hubert Humphrey 41.9 percent to 38.8 percent, with George Wallace receiving 5.6 percent. And a *CD* article noted that drug use at UVA was three years behind the nation in general. But, as it turned out, this was the lull before the storm. By spring semester, this period of calm would seem long in the past. And the first step in that direction surfaced during the second week of October.

## UVA's "Rosa Parks" Moment

I remember reading the story in *The Cavalier Daily* on October 8—how they had learned that one of the barber shops on the Corner had refused to cut the hair of a black youth, and how they had followed up by contacting all three of the Corner barbershops, with only one of them saying that they would cut a black person's hair. In my naiveté, I was greatly surprised. While the "don't go up to the balcony" incident was still strong in my memory, this was two years later, and I had believed the events in the intervening period, including the murder of Martin Luther King Jr., had at least put to rest acts of overt racism in the community. I had apparently been mistaken, and as the *CD* asserted, it was an outrage that this was happening "right under our noses." Right under our noses, indeed! These were establishments just steps from Mincers and The Virginian and were probably visited by most if not all of the student body and faculty at one time or another. The proximity of it all finally stirred both students and the administration into action. Students began calling for a boycott of discriminatory establishments, and within a week, the University administration agreed to officially join the students in boycotting such entities.

In response to the growing support of virtually all factions on Grounds, Student Council unanimously moved to support a boycott of all barbers and beauticians who discriminated on the basis of race, religion, or national origin. Today, looking at that action by the council, one would colloquially utter, "No duh." But at the time, it was a groundbreaking decision, and one that was recognized as such by the progressive editors of the *CD*:

> The Student Council's resolution encouraging a boycott by all University personnel of local establishments who refuse to serve any and all members of the University community regardless of race, color, religion or national origin is one of the boldest moves we have ever seen the Council take. Without doubt, it will prove one of the most controversial of its actions to date... The all-important distinction between this and other equally noble and conscientious actions of Council is attempting to impose its own thinking on elements of society at the University; in a broader sense, then, for the first time an official body of the University is, in the name of the University of Virginia, taking positive and obtrusive action to try to bring about social 'reform' in the community in which it is located.

It was in fact a bold move, and to appreciate it, one has to be reminded of the true state of the surroundings in which we lived in Charlottesville in the fall of 1968. In response to the actions at the University, most area barbers in effect thumbed their collective noses and refused to treat all potential customers equally. The representative of one of the barber shops on East Main Street was quoted as saying, "Students don't get many haircuts anyway. The troublemakers will all be gone in a few years... If a Negro comes into my store, I will tell him we don't need his business anyway." The failure to evoke a positive response from the local shops led to further threats of action from certain segments of the community. Only after plans were announced by the local chapter of the Council on Human Relations and by some

UVA students to picket the defiant establishments did some of the shops relent. And on October 21, all the barber shops on the Corner became open to all students at the University.

Following this landmark victory of sorts, things pretty much quieted down on the Grounds for the rest of the semester. Nary a peep was heard about the war, and UVA's continuing issues dealing with its civil rights legacy would not emerge in a material way again until the spring semester, when it would resurface with a bang.

## UVA's "Monty Python" Moment

Within days of the barber shop furor dying down, UVA was to witness what would be perhaps the greatest prank/hoax and moment of high camp in the history of the University. In 1968, the Mexico City Summer Olympics actually took place in the fall for only the third time in Olympic history. Opening ceremonies were held on October 12, and events were in full flow when a *Cavalier Daily* headline story on October 23 announced, "The Olympic flame—the real Olympic flame that is—is not at the Olympic Games in Mexico City, but in a hidden spot in Charlottesville." And thus began an outrageous tale that would dominate discussion and headlines on Grounds and would attain national prominence.

The gist of the story was that a group of editors from the *Rapier* magazine, UVA's new journal of satire, had hijacked the real Olympic torch en route to Mexico City from Mt. Olympus and substituted in its place a torch of their own. The convoluted tale included having had a group of engineers construct an exact replica of the torch, contacting a local who knew several of the runners carrying the torch from Veracruz to Mexico City, and convincing one of the runners to exchange the real torch for the *Rapier* replica for an undisclosed sum of money. The bizarre story continued with the claim that in order to get the true flame across the border, the real flame was transferred from the torch to a kerosene lantern, which was then driven to Charlottesville. The real torch was buried in Mexico, while the *Rapier* fake torch was lit by a Rapier editor's zippo lighter and carried to Mexico City.

Having allegedly sequestered the true Olympic flame in a hidden location in Cville, the perpetrators magnanimously offered to return it to the Mexican government as a gift on October 25, just prior to the closing ceremonies two days later. The plan was to have the flame carried by a series of runners beginning at the *Rapier's* offices on Rugby Road and ending at the Mexican Embassy in Washington D.C. Accordingly, the *Rapier* issued a request for runners, and within a day, sixty students answered the call. Despite the fact that the Mexican Embassy refused to cooperate and nixed a meeting with the *Rapier* editors, the first runner, Bob Cullen, then the Sports Editor of the *CD* and later to become its Editor-in-Chief, left the *Rapier* offices as planned on October 25. Amazingly, this event was covered by all three of the major TV networks at the time—ABC, NBC, and CBS. ABC actually followed the run from the air in a chartered plane. Not surprisingly, the event ended as expected—the Mexican ambassador refused to accept the "gift" and the flame fizzled.

*The last mile of the Olympic torch 'marathon'*

Preposterous as this may all seem now, the flame incident captured the attention and focus of practically everyone at UVA for a week in the fall of 1968—in the midst of one of the most contentious elections of the century and while student anti-war demonstrations sizzled at campuses across the country. Discussions ranged from whether it was a hoax to whether it was an honor offense, or at least behavior unbecoming a gentleman. As for myself, I found the whole series of events quite amusing. In my mind, it was undoubtedly a hoax, but a brilliantly conceived one nevertheless. In context, it was a more sophisticated version of stuffing students into a phone booth (when phone booths still existed). And in my mind, this was partly what college was all about. Particularly in October 1968, creative frivolity was a welcome respite from the vicissitudes of the increasingly disturbing real world.

## Two More Legends in the Classroom

At the end of the previous school year, I had to make two choices regarding my future academic career. First was choosing a major. I seriously considered both government and history, and in the end my lifelong passion for history won out.[42] Next, the option was open to me to apply for the history honors program. At that time, most of the social sciences offered an honors program pursuant to application and acceptance. The programs differed somewhat for each department. The history program was roughly based upon the British tutorial system— small seminars, independent research, a senior thesis and final-year written and oral exams. It sounded like an interesting change of pace to me, so I applied and was pleased to have been accepted.

In practice, the program worked as follows—third year you chose one of a number of honors seminars being offered each semester (which counted as nine credits) and supplemented each seminar with two regular courses each semester. Fourth year, the seminars each semester were supplemented by one course and the senior thesis. This was all

---

42  At that time, double majors were not in vogue. I knew no one with a double major.

supposed to be accompanied in theory by independent research. In any event, I chose my first honors seminar in the fall of 1968—a course entitled "American Radical and Reform Movements" (very apropos for the time period) taught by a young history professor, Joseph Kett.

Mr. Kett had arrived at UVA only two years before after having received his Ph.D. in history from Harvard and serving there as a self-proclaimed "junior flunky." As it turned out, this seminar was the single best course I would take in my academic career. And as it also turned out, this was part of the beginning of an illustrious career at UVA for Mr. Kett. He would teach for over four more decades at the University, much to the benefit and delight of thousands of UVA students. Mr Kett's U.S. history survey courses became a staple for liberal arts students. Famed Wahoo alum Katie Couric has been quoted as saying that Joe Kett was her favorite professor at UVA. And I was more than thrilled when my daughter had the privilege of taking his course and had the opportunity to listen to his rapid fire, incisive, and fascinating discourses on American history. But unfortunately for me, Mr. Kett's seminar set a standard for excellence that would not be equaled during my next three semesters in the honors program.

*Attending Mr. Kett's honor seminar in his living room, Fall 1968*

I was very lucky in my course selections my third year. Not only did I have my most stimulating course ever with Joe Kett, I also took my most enjoyable course ever. And that would be Shakespeare with the indomitable Dean of the College, Irby B. Cauthen (*see photo pg 40*). Dean Cauthen was truly the most perfect Virginia Gentleman and the epitome of the refined Southern scholar. Indeed, he was right out of central casting—impeccably attired, courteous, genteel, and cultured. But more than anything, it was his manner of speaking—that sublime voice, that rich, mellifluous, smooth Southern accent. Especially for a kid like me, who had grown up in New York City listening to the fast-paced, strident, hyper-nasal accent prevalent there, the soft, mellow, dulcet tones emanating from this scholar were mesmerizing. Forget about the content of the class, I would have paid the price of admission just to listen to Dean Cauthen vocalize the lines from Hamlet and King Lear.

Irby Cauthen had grown up in South Carolina and received his undergraduate degree from Furman. He attended UVA for his master's degree, but was interrupted by World War II, where he served in North Africa and Italy and won a Bronze Star. He returned from the war, finished his Ph.D. in English at the University, began his teaching career at Hollins College and then returned to Charlottesville as a professor. He became Dean of the College in 1962 and served in that capacity until 1978. Dean Cauthen continued to teach literature until his death in 1994. As was the case with his fellow dean, Braxton Woody, a first-year dorm was subsequently named for him. A fitting honor for an unforgettable figure in UVA history.

## *Election Night*

The 1968 presidential election was one of the most tumultuous in U.S history. Following the assassinations of Martin Luther King Jr. and Robert Kennedy, the attendant unrest and the turmoil at the Democratic Convention, it was predicted to be an extremely close finish between Richard Nixon and Hubert Humphrey, with Alabama

Governor George Wallace running a significant third-party campaign. With the Vietnam War still raging, numerous college campuses in rebellion, and many of our futures in doubt, there was an extraordinary amount of interest in the election within the student body, even extending to the white columns bordering Rugby Road and Mad Lane. I can remember going over to the AEPi house that evening and plunking myself down in our mixed party/dining room, which had been set up as a mini-theater, with the TV placed on the stage where the band usually played (unfortunately, no wide screens in 1968) and rows of chairs placed in front of it.

As predicted, election night turned out to be a nail biter, and as the evening wore on, more and more of the brothers and pledges joined the crowd in front of the tube. It was a lively group. While probably a large majority of the house was pulling for Humphrey, there were enough Nixon supporters present to make the ongoing commentary and dialogue vibrant and spirited. There was a constant stream of banter and ribbing going on as usual, and an occasional empty beer or cola can tossed in the direction of an ideological opponent—but it was all in good fun.

When I left the house about midnight to head back to McCormick Road, the result was still in doubt. And what I remember most about that evening was not the outcome of the election, but rather that I had spent the night with a buoyant and cheerful group of friends. Sure, most of us were keenly interested in who would win, and more than a few were intensely partisan, but the overwhelming spirit of the evening was that of camaraderie. At that point in time, friendship still took precedence over politics—at least at the Pi lodge. The fact that you had partied, gone down the road and dined daily with your buddy was more important than whether he was a Republican or Democrat, for or against the war, etc. Unfortunately, the fall of 1968 would by and large be the last time I could say that about my undergraduate experience at UVA. The cascading events of the following semester would cause an ever-widening divide not only at the AEPi house, but among various groups of students on Grounds. The great bond of sociability that had previously united most Wahoos was about to be rent asunder.

I woke up the next morning to learn that Richard Nixon had finally succeeded in coming back from his razor-thin loss to John Kennedy in 1960 and his embarrassing defeat in the 1962 California gubernatorial race. It seemed that the press would in fact have Dick Nixon to kick around some more. To me, the surprise was not Nixon's victory, but the extent of George Wallace's electoral success. The Alabama governor carried five Southern states—Alabama, Mississippi, Georgia, Louisiana and Arkansas—and received over thirteen percent of the popular votes nationwide. More importantly, in the context of this narrative and to put things in proper perspective, Wallace received over twenty-three percent of the vote in Virginia, and he and Nixon combined accounted for two thirds of the vote in the Old Dominion. Setting the landscape for the rest of this story, it is significant to remember how conservative a state Virginia was at that time.

## I Toss My Hat in the Ring

One of my heroes, Edmund Burke,[43] once said, "We must all obey the great law of change. It is the most powerful law of nature." But then Burke also stated, "When change is not necessary, it is necessary not to change." In essence, I believe this great statesman and political theorist was saying that while some change is always going to occur, let's not throw the baby out with the bathwater. And that was sort of my state of mind in mid-November 1968. While things were still fairly quiescent around the Grounds, particularly when compared to other college campuses, it was pretty clear that major changes were on the horizon. Although we were all waiting for Dean Woody's official report on coeducation, most of us realized that the prospect of coeds in Charlottesville, the most profound game changer, was no longer

---

43  This Irish-born author and philosopher was an eighteenth-century leader of the Whig Party in the British Parliament. He is probably most famous for being a supporter of the American Revolution and an opponent of the French Revolution.

an issue. The question was when and how, not if. Also, for the first time, University administrators appeared to be taking seriously UVA's deficient civil rights history. Moreover, many aspects of the Old U, including the Honor System and coats and ties, were being challenged in a manner and with a frequency that was unprecedented on Grounds. *The Cavalier Daily*, once again commenting on its favorite subject of "change," stated the following in its November 21 editorial entitled the "State of the University":

> The University seems to be taking on the appearance of a dramatically changing institution to the outside world… There is no doubt that the University is in a new era of change and challenge and that the institutions within it which have always been accepted without question are being questioned for the first time.

With all this in mind, I decided to run for Student Council in the fall elections. As noted previously, I was loving my time in Charlottesville. After over two years at the U, I fully understood the unique experience I was having compared to friends' experiences at other institutions. This had been particularly brought home to me after a trip that fall to visit one of my oldest and dearest friends, Steve Loeshelle, at Wesleyan University in Connecticut. It was a school I would have loved to have been able to get into as a high school student—but in 1968, I wouldn't have traded places given the opportunity. Yes, change was coming to UVA, but I hoped it would not materially damage those aspects of life at the University that made it such a special place—the Honor System, coats and ties, individual responsibility, student self governance, the collegiality and sociability that marked student interaction on Grounds, and that certain je ne sais quoi that made UVA "UVA." In my view, given that coeducation was a foregone conclusion, there was really only one area where material action needed to be taken— and that was UVA's shoddy civil rights history. No matter how you sliced and diced it, no matter what excuses were made, the University as a state institution had failed miserably in its obligations to its black citizenship. So ever mindful of Burke, this was truly one area where change was necessary.

Thus, being convinced that my remaining year and a half at UVA would be witness to a number of important and interesting issues and events, I submitted my name to the Sceptre Society for nomination to Student Council. At that time, running for student office from one of the caucuses was similar in many ways to running for public office from one of the two national political parties. I noted earlier how both Sceptre and Skull & Keys held a caucus to choose its candidates, and how important it was to build your support prior to the caucus. I therefore was out and about contacting my friends and key "politicos" in each fraternity to muster support for the caucus. As for those houses where I did not personally have contacts, I found friends who did, and they acted as my proxy in pushing my candidacy. The night of the caucus, each candidate gave a formal speech to the assembled crowd. I can clearly remember mounting the stage in Old Cabell Hall and delivering my speech, which I had assiduously worked on for hours. I had never addressed a formal crowd as large as this before, and the effort was both daunting and exhilarating. But, as I mentioned previously, the real work had been done before the gathering, and that had been good enough to get me successfully nominated.

The actual campaign would run for a number of weeks between Thanksgiving and Christmas holidays. And it was a campaign—posters went up, interviews were given to the *CD*, and numerous campaign talks were given in the McCormick Road dorms. The dorm talks were important, because first-years tended to vote at significantly higher levels than the upper classmen, cynicism not having yet set in. This was where it was quite helpful being a dorm counselor. You knew most of the other counselors, and you would go corridor to corridor asking each fellow counselor to gather his counselees in his room for your talk. It was effective, if also exhausting. But I knew I had to pull out all the stops if I was to be successful. While I felt confident in my ability to compete favorably with the other caucus candidates for the four council seats up for grabs, the recently surging University Party had nominated a particularly strong group of candidates, including Tony Sherman, the first black student to ever run for a council seat from the College.

Toward the end of the council campaign, the University administration issued two important announcements. First, it was revealed that the University had hired Fred Stokes, a graduate student in the Education School, to be the first black administrator for the admissions office. He was to be an assistant to Dean of Admissions Ernie Ern, with much of his work focused toward recruiting black students. At this point, the black undergraduate population had "ballooned" to twenty-two students. And then, a few days later, the University issued Dean Woody's long-awaited report on coeducation, eighteen months in the making. To no one's surprise at that point, the report supported the institution of coeducation at UVA, concluding, "If the University of Virginia at Charlottesville is to fulfill its function as the state university it must open its doors to all qualified citizens of the state without discrimination with respect to race, color, religion, national origin, or sex."

The balloting for Student Council took place on December 17 and 18, just before the Christmas break (remember, exams were not until after break). I did not find out the results until after I arrived home in New York. Over nineteen hundred votes had been cast in the College, and in a squeaker, I had come in fifth of the dozen candidates running, just sixteen votes behind the fourth-place candidate. Only one of the four winners was a caucus candidate. Three of the four victorious candidates were from the University Party, with Tony Sherman receiving the highest vote total by far. It was truly a new era on Grounds. The other two UP winners were also formidable candidates. Kevin Mannix would later be elected Student Council president and in the real world would become a state legislator in Oregon and run for governor of that state (surprisingly as a Republican). Ron Cass would later become the

Dean of Boston University Law School.

While I was disappointed, I felt I had run a good race in a difficult environment against impressive opponents. But what did trouble me was an event that had occurred just prior to the voting. It was an action that represented a breach of the unwritten rules of collegial student interaction at UVA and that would be a precursor of even worse to come. It was a "midnight" smear attack, and nothing like it had been seen in recent UVA history—or perhaps ever on Grounds. The event was subsequently addressed in a column by the Managing Editor of the *CD*, Rod McDonald, in which he criticized the use of the last-minute smear letter that had disparaged the caucus candidates. This personally struck home, as the column noted, "The idea was to attack the qualifications of the caucus candidates, the result was a major influence on the caucuses' loss, notably Joel Gardner's as he ran 17 [sic] scant votes behind the fourth candidate elected." While the smear letter attacked the caucus candidates as a group and did not mention individual candidates by name, this type of political assault that denigrated one's opponents had been unheard of on Grounds. It was not in the ethos of UVA—it was just not what "Virginia Gentlemen" did. But, then again, the days of the traditional Virginia Gentleman were coming to an end. A lesson I was beginning to learn the hard way.

## *The Bubble Bursts*

Although my initial foray into UVA electoral politics had ended unhappily, I returned to Charlottesville for second semester with a full plate before me. I would soon begin writing a column for *The Cavalier Daily*, an activity I very much looked forward to, particularly in the eventful times we were experiencing. I also had been elected the Lieutenant Master (vice-president) of AEPi, which meant I was the pledgemaster for the new pledge class. Since pledging lasted until the beginning of the next school year, it was a semester-long job.

Meanwhile, the new semester began with a series of significant events. First was the opening of Wilson Hall, which was the first new building to open in the Jeffersonian Grounds area since New Cabell Hall had opened in the early 1950s. This was followed by two announcements of progress in the civil rights arena—two black history courses were set to begin and black enrollment was anticipated to triple for the academic year of 1969-1970. And then came the much-anticipated promulgation on coeducation. In a statement entitled "Resolution on the Admission of Women Adopted by the Board of Visitors of the University of Virginia on 15 February 1969," the University announced that full coeducation would begin on Grounds in the fall of 1970—thus making my class the last class at UVA to graduate prior to coeducation. But none of the above developments would define the spring semester—the real story of the spring of 1969 was about to unfold simultaneously with the coeducation announcement on February 17, 1969.

It had all started a few days earlier, when local members of the Students for a Democratic Society ("SDS"), probably the most influential of the radical national student organizations, launched an attack on the Board of Visitors. Denigrating the BOV as a group of white, upper-middle-class businessmen (no doubt true to a great extent), the SDS requested the governor to appoint a board that would be representative of the ethnic, economic, and social nature of the state. The SDS also singled out BOV member C. Stuart Wheatley as a focal point of the attack. Wheatley, as a state legislator from Danville, had been a major proponent of the "massive resistance" movement in Virginia a decade earlier. The SDS called for Wheatley's resignation as well as action by the "elitist" board to undo the effects of years of integration neglect. In and of itself, the SDS's actions would probably not have amounted to much. Most Wahoos either didn't really know much about the SDS, or if they did know, didn't care. The local SDS members were mostly considered outliers, radicals, and agitators (again, no doubt true to a great extent). But then an individual emerged who would instigate a series of actions that succeeded in giving at least part of the SDS agenda a cloak of respectability—and that person was Robert Rosen. He wasn't the

President of Student Council or the Chair of the Honor Committee, and he didn't hold any other elective office, but in February 1969, Robert Rosen's actions would arguably change the course of UVA history as much, if not more, than any single student ever had or ever would.

Robert Rosen was a fourth-year student from Charleston, South Carolina, and was a well-known figure around the Grounds. He was a founding editor of the *Rapier* magazine, a regular contributor to *The Cavalier Daily*, and a Lawn resident. I happened to know Robert fairly well, as he was a "social member" of AEPi—meaning he ate some meals with us and attended our parties, but was not a brother. Although Robert and I disagreed on a number of things, I always had great respect for his intelligence, which was manifest. He was clearly the intellectual fountainhead of liberalism at UVA at that time. One only had to read his liberal manifesto, "A Prospectus for the University," published in the *CD* the previous September, to have realized that here was an intellect and a person to be taken seriously. Thus, Robert Rosen had been the foremost liberal apostle in a traditionally conservative milieu—and in February 1969, events finally caught up with his preaching.

There is an old saying, "Timing is everything." Hyperbole perhaps, but timing can be incredibly important, particularly when you have the right individual or individuals perceptive enough to recognize that the time is ripe for action. And why was February 1969 the right time? Well, as we have seen, 1968 was a traumatic year overall for our country, and at UVA the winds of change had been blowing slowly but surely for over a year. The barbershop incident in the fall had finally shocked UVA out of its civil rights hibernation, and college campuses across the nation were in rebellion. In fact, early February had witnessed major student disturbances at many colleges, including Duke, where a nine-hour student rebellion marked the first major college uprising in the South. So it was at this propitious moment in history that Robert Rosen convened a meeting in his room on the Lawn on Sunday, February 16. It was at this meeting that the Student Coalition was born, and things would not quite be the same on Grounds henceforth—the "bubble" had burst.

The Student Coalition was comprised of a broad array of student leaders, ranging from left-wing Student Council members like Walker Chandler and T. Jackson Lears to traditional fraternity leaders like Ed Hayes (IFC president), George Shipley (University Union president), Ron Hickman (Student Council president), and Rick Evans (prior Student Council president). These "Old U" fraternity men came from some of the most "Southern" and "preppy" houses on Grounds, such as KA, SAE and St. Anthony's Hall. There could be no doubt that this was truly a diverse group of Wahoos. The key, as expressed by various coalition leaders, was to clearly demonstrate that the forthcoming actions of the coalition did not represent the activities of wide-eyed radicals and agitators and that support for stronger actions to address the racial issues at the University was widespread amongst the student body.

After the meeting in Rosen's room, the coalition moved quickly to implement its goals. Another meeting was held on the Lawn the next day to prepare a list of proposals and demands to be presented to the University community. An eleven-point program was adopted, including proposals making the University application fee optional for low-income students, making the then mandatory application photo optional, securing the appointment of a full-time black assistant dean of admissions, increasing the minimum wage for non-academic employees, giving University employees the right to organize, and having the governor agree to make all future BOV appointments with the aim of having the board's composition brought into line with the racial, gender, and age make-up of the state population. Interestingly, the coalition's eleven-point manifesto contained many of the same proposals being advanced by the SDS and the SSOC. Indeed, Rosen was quoted as saying the SDS was right some of the time. Well, at least for the first few days, the bridge between the SDS and Rugby Road was holding. The editors of the *CD* were ecstatic (the Editor-in-Chief of the *CD*, Richard Gwathmey, being a supporter of the coalition). On the day the eleven-point program was promulgated, an editorial entitled "Leaders on the Lawn" stated, "Those who will gather on Mr. Jefferson's Lawn today are not hippies, weirdos or misfits in any sense. They are rather the representatives and members of the student establishment of the University... They are products of 150 years of carefully preserved traditionalism. They are rational idealists who have finally been moved to constructive action by mounting frustration."

The following day would be the pinnacle of the coalition's cohesion and support. Over a thousand students turned out on the Lawn to listen to coalition leaders, faculty, and members of the community speak in support of the eleven proposals. Rosen spoke, as did SDS leader Steve Squire (allegedly speaking only on behalf of himself). Mrs. Willie Lee Rose, assistant professor of history, told the crowd, "The faculty will stand behind you if you are responsible in your efforts." Rev. David Ward of St. Paul's Episcopal Church and Rev. Howard Gordon of the United Ministries added their support. But, perhaps most telling were the comments by graduate Student Council member Bud Ogle, who stated, "We must be willing to go anywhere, any time, to do anything and everything necessary to get these minimum prerequisites." And there was the rub—the invocation to "do anything and everything."

I remember that demonstration on the Lawn well. It was a cold and blustery February day. There was a huge turnout—but not everyone was a supporter. Many turned out because it was a happening—an event certainly not seen before in recent memory. And after listening to Steve Squire and Bud Ogle speak, I knew that the days of the Student Coalition being a true "coalition" were numbered. While many students on Grounds were united behind at least some, if not all, of the eleven points, most were not willing to "do anything and everything" to attain them; and thus the means of achieving those ends would ultimately be the rock on which this wave would break.

*[L-R] Ron Cass, Robert Rosen, and George Taylor at the Lawn Student Coalition rally*

The first major issue that would divide the coalition was how to approach the C. Stuart Wheatley matter. The left wing of the coalition was adamantly pushing for his resignation, or at a minimum, an open apology for his behavior in support of segregation a decade earlier. But anyone familiar with Virginia politics and the state of the Commonwealth at that time knew that such demands would fall on deaf ears. The governor, Mills Godwin, was a conservative Byrd Democrat, and the Old Dominion had proved its conservative credentials in the recent presidential election. The more moderate members of the coalition were happy with a confirmation from Mr. Wheatley that he had changed his views. And that is exactly what happened. Student Council President Ron Hickman, a traditional student leader, had a conversation with Mr. Wheatley in which Wheatley asserted that his opinions had changed and that he intended to see that all students have an equal opportunity to attend UVA. In a letter to the University community, Hickman noted that he believed that Wheatley was truly concerned with the issue of equal opportunity and asserted, "I would hope that students would direct their efforts, as a result, towards more productive goals, such as helping to realize greater numbers of Black students at the University of Virginia." Thus, there was a real divide as to how far to push this issue. Some continued to demand Wheatley's resignation and collected a petition with over eight hundred signatures in furtherance of the cause. Others saw this as a confrontational distraction from achievable goals. In any event, this effort eventually went nowhere. Student Council rejected a motion asking for Wheatley's resignation, and while it later passed a resolution urging Wheatley to publicly repudiate the principles behind massive resistance, the council at the end of the day would accept a statement from Wheatley that was less than a repudiation and more in line with what he had stated to Ron Hickman weeks earlier.

Another area that divided the coalition concerned its interactions with President Shannon. Any person who was lucky enough to know Edgar Finley Shannon knew that this scholar of nineteenth-century Victorian literature was an eminently intelligent and reasonable man. He was open minded and flexible, and clearly not in the mold of Mills Godwin or Stuart Wheatley. And, while I am pretty sure that this Rhodes Scholar and World War II naval officer never imagined he would be in this position when he accepted the UVA presidency, I believe he was genuinely sympathetic to many of the coalition's goals. That is why the confrontational approach that many leaders of the coalition took vis a vis President Shannon further fractured the coalition and turned many students against it, if not all of its objectives.

The coalition had submitted its manifesto to President Shannon during the February 18 demonstration and requested an immediate response. He responded a week later, stating that he supported efforts to raise the wages of University employees and favored an institution that was totally non-discriminatory on racial grounds. However, there was no discussion on specific actions to be taken immediately. Well, this response did not play well with the activists. The coalition roundly criticized President Shannon, called for a public debate with him and asserted that it was committed to applying continuing pressure until its objectives were realized. Another demonstration was called for on March 4, and the coalition leaders demanded that the president engage them in a face-to-face dialogue. The confrontational tone of this response turned off many members of the University community. Even *The Cavalier Daily*, an avid supporter of the coalition, was prompted to say that while one could be disappointed with President Shannon's response, one should not be indignant.

*President and Mrs. Shannon at Carr's Hill*

The disappointment with the coalition's methods was probably best expressed by George McMillan[44], a Law School Student Council rep-

---

44  George McMillan would later serve as a progressive legislator and lieutenant governor of Alabama. He would just miss being elected governor, losing to George Wallace by a hair in the 1982 Democratic gubernatorial primary, which marked Wallace's final comeback effort.

resentative who was widely viewed as an influential student leader on Grounds:

> The goals of the student protests which have been reg-
> istered at the University during the past two weeks are
> laudable, but the tactics being used to achieve them
> are futile if not downright destructive. If continued,
> the tactics will thwart rather than expedite the achieve-
> ment of the goals they support. On the one hand the
> student protesters have demonstrated in a peaceful and
> orderly manner, but on the other they have demon-
> strated an intolerance for those who hesitate to express
> their goals with the same degree of vociferousness... In
> an attempt to accomplish anything, one must take into
> consideration the people with whom one is dealing.

The March 4 demonstrations and speeches took place, but this time to a much-reduced crowd. This would be the last major demonstration held by the Student Coalition, although their activities continued for a few more weeks, with the last significant event being a meeting on March 12 between coalition leaders and Governor Godwin.[45] From a practical point of view, the meeting was a complete failure. After the meeting, the governor said that he did not support the goals of the coalition and that he would in no way work for change in any of Virginia's policies dealing with the bargaining power for employees, increased wages, the composition of the BOV or any type of desegrega-tion plan. He noted that the students, either because of "inexperience" or "immaturity," did not understand the complexities of government and that their place at UVA was for education and not social protest. Quite a smackdown, no matter how you looked at it—proving George McMillan's point that one has to take into account who one is dealing with. And here the coalition was dealing with a conservative Byrd-

---

45  Although, as we shall see, there was a final hurrah at the Sesquicentennial celebrations a month later.

machine governor, in a conservative state, in a heated national atmosphere plagued by college disruptions.

Thus, while the Student Coalition did not witness any immediate material successes, it was a signal event in the history of the University. First and foremost, it set the stage for increased student activism at UVA, which would come to a head the following year and which would continue in one form or another well into the 1970s. This is not to say that the Grounds were radicalized or even that a majority of the students supported the coalition. In fact, a contemporaneous student poll had found that over sixty percent had little or no fact orientation regarding the coalition and that most could not name any of the coalition leaders. But clearly, the days were over of UVA being a sleepy, inward-looking institution, wallowing in its own traditions. Pretty much everything was now open to challenge and change—and such challenge and change would come sooner rather than later.

In addition, while neither the governor nor President Shannon offered immediate concessions to the coalition's demands, many of those demands would be addressed in some fashion in a relatively short time frame. The coalition made it clear to all on Grounds that racial inequality was no longer an acceptable M.O. at UVA. It is still astonishing to me decades later that all at once you had leaders of the most Southern and patrician fraternities coming together and in a loud voice saying, "no mas."

Another key point is that the impetus and energy for the demonstrations all came from the students. Despite Professor Rose's comments at the initial demonstration on the Lawn, the UVA faculty never really supported the coalition. In fact, the faculty senate decided to defer debate on the coalition's proposals only a day after Rose spoke.

This lack of faculty support was not really surprising at that time. The political make-up of college faculties in the 1960s was materially different than at present. Numerous studies over the past two decades have shown that college faculties have become increasingly liberal. Some of the findings are astounding, such as the one that found that as to those professors from the eight Ivy League schools who made donations in the 2012 presidential election, ninety-six percent went to Obama. Not a lot of thought diversity there. But that was not the case in 1969, when there were significant numbers of moderates and conservatives on college faculties, particularly at UVA, who were not amenable to student agitation. This reality was reflected in a contemporaneous *CD* story, which stated, "As universities across the country are being swept up in student turmoil, activists find more and more of their professors deserting them... New York University Professor Sidney Hook is touring the country persuading faculty members to bolster institutional defenses against the activist demands."

A further fascinating observation about the coalition and those historic weeks in February and March was the virtual absence of the anti-war issue. In the spring of 1969, colleges across the country were in turmoil, and the issue that fanned those flames of discord was the Vietnam War. But not at UVA. In Charlottesville, the sole focus of the demonstrations that, at least initially, brought so many factions together in an unprecedented manner was an attempt to right wrongs that were specific to the UVA experience. It was not part of the ever-expanding national anti-war protest movement—that would come the following year.

## *The Night They Drove Old Dixie Down*[46]

While the coalition's actions did not evoke an immediate response to its enumerated demands, its activities did result in some immediate "collateral damage." On February 25, the Student Council in a thirteen to five vote passed a resolution urging the University Band and UVA's student radio station, WUVA, to refrain from playing "Dixie" in the future. As noted earlier, "Dixie" was still the University Band's fight song of choice to rally the crowd at sporting events. And WUVA still had a practice of signing on and off with the anthem of the old

---

46 With compliments to The Band and Levon Helm. "The Night They Drove Old Dixie Down" was in fact recorded in 1969.

Confederacy. At the Student Council meeting, the Anarchist impresario Walker Chandler stated, "'Dixie' is a remnant of redneck society that refuses to die in spite of the number of times it has been kicked." Not the most sensitive or diplomatic statement—but to the point and symptomatic of a growing tendency to substitute restrained and cordial discourse with intemperate name-calling.

It took only a day after the Student Council action for the WUVA Board of Directors to call an impromptu meeting, agree that "Dixie" was an "anachronistic holdover" and decide to eliminate that standard from its daily repertoire. The University Band's use of "Dixie," however, did not terminate so quickly. "Dixie" could still be heard at football games the following fall, but, subjected to increasing condemnation, the band also banished that old rallying song of the South shortly thereafter.

But the death of "Dixie" at UVA did not come without protest. Many voices derided the attack on "Dixie," arguing that it was a source of regional pride and not meant as a racist anthem. The *CD* noted that the Student Council resolution "has been received somewhat less than favorably in many quarters… We have never before received so many letters from such a diverse group of people on any particular subject." I knew quite a few folks greatly agitated by this perceived attack on their Southern heritage. But in the end, the emotions unleashed by the Student Coalition in fact drove old "Dixie" down.

In my view, the success in ending the presence of "Dixie" on Grounds can be attributed to the fact that it was a "soft" target, in that it was entirely a student-controlled decision. No administration or faculty support was necessary to take this action—another example of the students leading the way in this sphere.

## An Unsettling Sesquicentennial

As we approach the University's Bicentennial in 2019, it is somewhat daunting for this author to be writing about the events surrounding the last similar celebration in Charlottesville, UVA's Sesquicentennial festivities, which took place almost fifty years ago on April 14, 1969. I remember the day well, as I was privileged to be a participant in the ceremonial procession down the Lawn, having been awarded Intermediate Honors.[47] It was a beautiful spring day, and following the Lawn processional, members of the University community filed into Old Cabell Hall for a series of speeches and awards honoring Mr. Jefferson and the founding of his University. A year of planning had gone into preparing for this celebration. But one thing the planners had not bargained for was the upheaval caused by the Student Coalition, and the aftermath of that upheaval was about to rain on their parade.

The day had begun somewhat ominously. *The Cavalier Daily*'s Sesquicentennial issue hit the stands with a split headline, "Celebration Surveys Feature Praise, Criticism." On one side was a column by William Willis, the director of Sesquicentennial events, discussing the cooperation, goodwill, and enthusiasm that had gone into planning the celebratory events. On the other side was an unsigned column by a member of the Student Coalition calling for a "counter-Founder's Day." The author encouraged coalition supporters to participate in events "in the manner he deems most appropriate to our goals." These proposed actions included boycotting or picketing events and walking out of Cabell Hall during the ceremonies—even though the author recognized that "some of our actions may be construed to be impolite or inconsiderate."

I was not surprised by the prominence afforded the front page anonymous coalition column, given the *CD*'s overwhelming support for the coalition. But things seemed to have quieted down somewhat over the past few weeks, and I really did not expect to see a lot of inappropriate behavior at the festivities. My instincts seemed to be correct as the Lawn processional proceeded without any significant protests and only limited picketing. However, midway through the program in

---

47  As noted earlier, Intermediate Honors was awarded to those students who had accrued a 3.2 GPA over their first four semesters. There were ninety-nine students out of over nine hundred who achieved this. My understanding is that today, a 3.2 GPA at UVA would not even put one in the top half of the class.

Old Cabell, while President Shannon was in the process of presenting a Seven Society humanitarian award for work in achieving social justice, somewhere between two hundred to three hundred people stood up and walked out of the auditorium. Well, I don't know about anyone else, but I was shocked. Sure, the coalition column had proposed walking out of Old Cabell auditorium, but at most I thought that might lead to a few students bolting from the ceremonies. I don't think anyone had anticipated a coordinated effort of this magnitude. And with this act of protest and certainly "impolite" and "inconsiderate" behavior, I believe the coalition lost a considerable amount of its remaining support. Up to that point, the increasingly strident nature of the coalition's actions had caused many of its moderate leaders to withdraw their support—a situation that I had noted in one of my *CD* columns, along with the observation that the Sesquicentennial protests were "more marked by beards and sandals than coats and ties." Even the *CD* noted that the timing of the protesters actions was "terrible" since it occurred during a presentation of an award supporting social justice. In any event, this would be the last hurrah for the coalition as a formal entity. However, as we shall see, much of the spirit of the coalition would carry on in the formation of a new student political party within a few weeks of the Sesquicentennial celebration.

The Sesquicentennial walk-out demonstrated just how far student activism had blossomed at UVA in such a short period. This action was certainly not the behavior of "Virginia Gentlemen," and would have been inconceivable a year, or perhaps even six months, earlier. The lines between the Old U and the New U were being drawn. This sharp contrast was illuminated in that same Sesquicentennial *Cavalier Daily* issue noted above, which contained both several coalition-sponsored articles calling for change and an article in which Dean Runk reminisced about his forty years at UVA. When asked whether the Old U was a better place, Dean Runk simply stated, "No question about it"— a sentiment shared by many others at that time.

*That's me marching in the 1969 Sesquicentennial procession—*
*notice the demonstrators in the background*

## *Boot the Hoot*

In the midst of the Student Coalition turmoil, another rebellion was brewing on Grounds in a most unlikely venue. On March 11, the *CD* reported that five UVA basketball players would be meeting that evening with basketball coach Bill "Hoot" Gibson and athletic director Steve Sebo to discuss complaints regarding Gibson that had been prepared by the team in a private meeting. The players representing the team—Chip Case, John English, Mike Wilkes, Norm Carmichael, and Tony Kinn—were basically the varsity starting five.

The first hint of problems on the hardcourt came a few days earlier when the Cavaliers were once again shown an early door at the ACC Tournament in Charlotte, North Carolina. After losing the opening-round game, several of the team's players had been arrested for "scalping" tickets at the tournament (a matter which was referred to the Judiciary Committee) and some had also spoken openly to the press about problems on the team. Prior to the meeting on the 11th, the team representatives had issued a statement apologizing for this behavior. However, while regretting that certain players had spoken to the press, they noted that there existed "justifiable grievances." These grievances, which had caused a breakdown in team morale, allegedly included offering scholarships and then reneging on the offers, and ignoring ballots for the team captaincy.

This story set off a frenzy of controversy, not only in Charlottesville, but across the Commonwealth. Almost immediately, "Boot the Hoot" buttons appeared on Grounds, and newspapers across the state took up the players' cause. In a headline entitled "Gibson Must Go," a *CD* sports columnist called for the Hooter's dismissal, citing several instances of top recruits who had left UVA's hoops program due to Gibson's actions. I was quite familiar with the team and knew a few of the players fairly well. As a New York City kid in the 1950s and 1960s, I was a natural college basketball fan, and had spent many an hour with my brother watching college hoops at the old Madison Square Garden on Eighth Avenue and 50th Street. I transferred this passion to Charlottesville and was one of the few Wahoos to attend most home games. Hell, back then you could show up at U Hall ten minutes before a game and sit mid-court in the lower section. I knew Tony Kinn from the dorms our first-year—he was one of the finest pure shooters to ever attend UVA. He had been the team's leading scorer the year before, averaging eighteen points a game (in the pre-three-point-shot era). And two first-year players were counselees on my corridor in Kent House. So I felt fairly invested in the controversy and sympathized with the players' grievances. Those sympathies were supported by the fact that UVA had experienced another losing season (10-13) and was then 50-97 under Gibson's tutelage.

But in the end, it didn't matter what I, the *CD*, or the players thought. Apparently, the powers-that-be at the University were no more willing to take bold action in the sports arena than they were in the halls of academia. Despite the meetings and the grievances, Gibson remained as coach, and the following month he dismissed from the team two of his more vocal critics—Tony Kinn and John English. So the Hooter was in and two past starting guards were out.

In retrospect, perhaps the powers-that-be knew what they were doing. While the 'Hoos would have a losing record once again the following season (10-15), they would stun the second-seeded Tar Heels 95-93 in the opening round of the 1970 ACC Tournament and then lose by one point to third-seeded NC State the following day. In 1970-1971, with the coming of Barry Parkhill, the Cavs would record their first winning season (15-11) in over a decade, and as previously noted, would win over twenty games the following year for the first time since 1928 and go to their first post-season tournament in school history. "Hoot" Gibson would be named the ACC Coach of the Year that season.

## *An Unwelcome "Welcome"*

Spring break couldn't come soon enough after all the turmoil engulfing Charlottesville in February and March 1969. In my prior two years at UVA, I had returned home to NYC for spring break, and I felt this was as good a time as any to take the traditional spring break road trip down to the Florida beaches. Accordingly, I got together with my two good buddies, Steve Hayes and Steve Brickman, and planned a journey down to Miami Beach. Our fellow counselor, Duane Moats, joined our little band as we piled into my Chevy Nova and headed down south on Route 95.

As we crossed the Virginia line, I will never forget what greeted us as we entered the Tar Heel state. There was a large billboard featuring a Ku Klux Klansman holding a flaming cross on a rampant stallion with the "greeting," "Welcome to North Carolina." This was accompanied by the ominous invocation, "You are in the Heart of Klan Country," followed by the request to "Help Fight Integration and Communism."

All of us in the car were understandably astounded by this. I was amazed—I had spent the past two years driving all over the state of Virginia and had never seen the likes of that. This was disconcerting to say the least—particularly since our car contained two Jews, a Catholic, and a Mormon. With the memories of Schwerner, Goodman, and Chaney[48] still fresh in my mind, and discretion being the better part of valor, I decided to slow down and make sure I did not exceed the speed limit as we traveled through the "Heart of Klan Country." No need to tempt fate.

*KKK billboard in North Carolina—this could have been the one we saw*

Fortunately, we did pass through North Carolina without incident; but the picture of that hooded Klansman on his unbridled mount will forever be branded in my memory—along with the concept that this type of nonsense was still being openly displayed in America in 1969.

---

48   The three civil rights workers murdered with Klan participation in Neshoba County, Mississippi, in 1964.

## Not Just Another Election

After spring break, all eyes on Grounds turned to the election for the President of the College. As noted previously, this position was synonymous with being the Chairman of the Honor Committee—the most prestigious student office at the University. Traditionally, this had been pretty much a popularity contest, as the Honor System had been considered "above politics" and there usually was very little difference in substance between the candidates' views on the system. The major differences were whether the candidate was a Zete, a Hallie, a Deke, etc.; an Eli or a T.I.L.K.A.; a Z or an IMP. But, as with many things at UVA, this was no longer the case in the spring of 1969.

The two caucuses predictably nominated two traditional candidates. I knew both candidates reasonably well, as both were fellow counselors. The Sceptre Society chose Greg Hodges, a KA (Kappa Alpha Order) from Alabama, which was somewhat of a surprise as he had not been viewed as one of the leading candidates. On the other hand, Skull & Keys nominated Whitt Clement, one of the acknowledged leaders of our class. On paper, Whitt was classic Old U—multi-generational Virginian, Episcopal High School, Phi Kap. But anyone who knew Whitt knew he was more of a regular guy than anything else. He had a quick wit (no pun intended), a sparkling personality and was even-handed and open-minded. He was early on considered to be the stronger of the caucus candidates. But the factor that made this election a very different affair than those in the past was the entrance into the race of Charlie Murdock, the erstwhile Anarchist Student Council member. With that, the contest suddenly became very political. As the *CD* put it, this election matched the "standard bearers of the old guard against the anarchist champion of the New Left."

Not surprisingly, the Honor Code had not emerged unscathed from the tumult of the prior few months. The movement for change unleashed by the Student Coalition soon encompassed the Honor System, which was viewed by some as perhaps the greatest shibboleth of the Old U. Murdock deemed it a "racist" institution and part of the old genteel boys' club. He proposed that the system's procedures be more like a public courtroom trial and wanted the cheating prohibition limited to academic matters only and the stealing prohibition limited to its occurrence within the University community. Others went further and called for limiting the system to academic cheating only, ending the "lying and stealing part of the trinity."

These proposals and others clearly represented the most extensive assault launched against the Honor System in generations. They represented not merely suggestions as to defining specific areas of scope, i.e. should the system apply to lying about one's age to get a beer, or questioning whether the system could efficiently be administered with a 24/7 national geographic scope. Rather, these criticisms went to the heart of whether the University could and should foster a community of honor and trust that transcended just academic matters. For myself and many others, this was the core of what made UVA such a special and unique place. We as a University community shared the commitment to not lie, cheat, or steal. It went far beyond just not cheating on an exam or lying to a professor about why an assignment was late. It meant not cheating a fellow student or local businessperson. It meant not lying to an administrator or local law enforcement officer. It meant there was an indelible bond of trust among those living in Mr. Jefferson's University and our neighbors in the community.

But Murdock's proposals went far beyond limiting the Honor System to the academic arena. Just as importantly, or even more so, he wanted to totally redefine the role of the President of the College. As noted earlier, historically the only role of the President of the College was as Chair of the Honor Committee. Murdock clearly and vociferously objected to this limited role for the College president. He believed that the president should actively join with other student leaders and push for social change on issues other than honor. In other words, he advocated politicizing the office—an office which at that time sat as both participating judge and jury at honor trials.

At this time, I had already begun my stint as a columnist for *The Cavalier Daily*, and it gives me great pleasure to be able to quote from my column of April 9, 1969, which dealt with this point. Almost fifty years later, I wouldn't change a word:

> In addition to challenging the scope of the Honor System, Mr. Murdock has challenged the nature of the position of the President of the College itself. He believes that the President, 'as the highest elected representative of the University's largest school', must take an activist position and become involved in University political affairs. According to the candidate, the President should not confine his efforts to the Honor Committee, but should actively join the crusade to right all the egregious wrongs that burden the University.
>
> Mr. Murdock is here advocating a policy that could be exceedingly important in this election. The position of President of the College is synonymous with that of Chairman of the Honor Committee... If we start electing the Chairman of the Honor Committee according to the candidate's views on the transition program, C. Stuart Wheatley, and the advisability of playing Dixie, then the Honor System will irrevocably suffer. An individual's political beliefs have absolutely no relevance to his position on the Honor Committee. And selecting an individual as Chairman according to his political beliefs can only work to the detriment of the Honor System by subordinating questions of honor to questions of politics.

I felt that way then and I feel that way now. Honor knows no party or ideology. Well, I guess quite a few of my fellow Wahoos agreed with me, because the result of the election was a blowout. Clement received 1,087 votes, Murdock 849, and Hodges 501. Thus, the "traditional" candidates received almost two thirds of the votes. But more impressive than the size of the victory, was the size of the turnout. The number of students voting broke a record—with over twenty-four hundred casting a ballot, representing over a seventy percent turnout. Quite astounding, particularly for a school known for its apathy and indifference. Why did this happen? Fortunately for the historian, I addressed this in my column analyzing the election results:

> Why the sudden burst of interest? What instigated the habitually apathetic Cavalier to take his mind off Easters Weekend, grain and debauchery, and cast his vote in the election? The answer is that for the first time in many a year, the students felt as if they were making a critical decision. They understood that they were not being confronted with a choice between a tweedledum and tweedledee; and realized the significant ramifications of their final decision. For the student body knew that this time the most important consideration was not whether the new President of the College was to be a KA or a Phi Kap—but whether the whole scope of the Honor System was to be saliently altered. The candidacy of Charles Murdock blatantly challenged the traditional concepts of the scope of the Honor System and the role of the President of the College.

So while in the spring of 1969 many a Cavalier was willing to embrace real change in some areas, there still existed a substantial "silent majority" that was not willing to accept significant change in the one area that still united most Wahoos—the Honor System. This did not mean, however, that the status quo was entirely acceptable. The Honor Committee was canny enough to understand that there was an important level of unrest regarding the system on Grounds, and within a month of the election, announced two changes to the code that, at least on the surface, appeared significant.

First, the committee announced that the system would be limited to activities related to student life at the University—this was rather broadly defined as all actions of a student in Charlottesville and Albemarle County as well as other situations where reliance was placed on the identity of an individual as a UVA student. In actuality, this was more of a recognition of the realities of recent history. While the Honor System in theory encompassed a 24/7 worldwide scope, the Honor Committee had not been called upon for years to try a case that entailed actions outside of Albemarle County. Thus, the concept of a community of honor among all students and their neighbors was preserved. Second, the committee declared that the prohibition of lying about one's age to obtain alcoholic refreshment would no longer be followed. This prohibition had been in effect only since 1956, and the committee deemed it no longer supportable. I guess the lure of a bourbon or a brew bested the collective instinct and agreement to tell the truth to local proprietors.

And as for our new Honor Chair, Whitt Clement, he would go on to become one of the most distinguished alums of our generation. He served as a highly regarded bipartisan member of the Virginia House of Delegates, was Secretary of Transportation under Governor Warner and is currently a member of the University's Board of Visitors. More importantly to me, he has been one of my dearest friends for the past five decades. If there is a more decent and honorable man around, I've yet to meet him.

## The End of Innocence

As we headed into the home stretch of spring semester and Student Council elections loomed on the horizon, the remnants of the Student Coalition licked their wounds over Charley Murdock's defeat in the College presidency election and decided to funnel their energies into the creation of a new organization. And thus was born the first student political party based on ideology rather than fraternity/independent status. Originally calling itself the "New Party," the group announced its existence on October 1. Founders of the New Party included such leaders of the Coalition as Bud Ogle, Ron Cass and Tom Gardner of the SSOC. Its first president was my classmate and fraternity brother, Bruce Wine.

The New Party shortly thereafter changed its name to the Virginia Progressive Party (VPP) and set out to actively recruit members. Its self-declared targets were moderate, liberal and "even radical" students. With the VPP's advantage of inheriting many, if not most, of the supporters of the coalition, including a number of the leaders of the University Party, the days of the UP were numbered. Some of the UP supporters attempted to keep the party alive, but it quickly folded, leaving the VPP as the united alternative to the desiccated fraternity caucuses.

As the nominating caucuses for Student Council were upon us, I was approached by several colleagues asking me to run again. While the caucus candidates had just won the College officer elections, I was fully aware of the dichotomy that had developed in student voting—traditionalist on honor, change on pretty much everything else. Thus, I knew that in the current atmosphere, running for Student Council from the caucuses would pretty much be a "forlorn hope."[49] Nevertheless, knowing that someone had to fight the good fight and that leadership often involves risks, I decided to enter the fray once again. The fact that my buddy Steve Hayes had also decided to run and that we were joined in the caucuses by two second-year men that I highly respected—Bill Fryer and Don Martin—made my decision easier. I still retain a copy of the Sceptre Society campaign poster in the Gardner Archives—with the young and nattily attired Hayes, Gardner, and Fryer looking out confidently at the electorate. I am proud to say that decades later, all in that group are still heavily invested in the welfare of the University. Indeed, Bill Fryer, who would later become my law school classmate

---

49 A "forlorn hope" is a military term that became popular in the eighteenth and nineteenth centuries and referred to those who volunteered to be in the first wave attacking a breach in an enemy's defenses during a siege. Most were killed, and those who survived received immediate promotions.

and a great friend forevermore, is today one of the most dedicated and effective alumni leaders at the University. He has served as a member of the College and Law School Foundations, the Chair of the Council of Foundations (or, as I refer to that position, the *capo di tutti capi*) and has been a confidante of many of the administrative leaders of the University who have been wise enough to seek his counsel.

## SCEPTRE SOCIETY
### COLLEGE ELECTIONS
## STUDENT COUNCIL

*Responsive Leadership For Progress*

**STEVE HAYES**

Dean's List; Pi Delta Epsilon; President, Sceptre Society; Dormitory Counselor; Managing Editor, Corks & Curls Treasurer, PK Dance Society; University Union Program Board; Student Council Concert Study Committee; IFC Representative, Sigma Phi Epsilon.

**JOEL GARDNER**

Dean's List; Phi Phi Sigma; Intermediate Honors; History Honors; Dormitory Counselor; Political Editor, UVM; Columnist, The Cavalier Daily; Rugby Club; IM Manager, Pledgemaster, President, Alpha Epsilon Pi.

**BILL FRYER**

Dean's List; Echols Scholar; Phi Eta Sigma; ACC Honor Roll Dormitory Counselor; German Club; Scholarship Committee IFC; Varsity Swimming; Vice President, Kappa Sigma.

*Student Council election poster, Spring 1969*

In any event, both caucuses combined had a fairly impressive array of candidates, but it would not be enough to withstand the tide for change that swept aside all but the Honor Code. The only caucus candidate to win a seat was Steve Hayes, who was not only a long-standing leader of our class and a great guy, but was helped both by his brother Ed being a hero of the coalition and, as the *CD* noted, by his playing the "liberal hand" well, running to the left of the rest of the caucus candidates. It was a great victory for the VPP and would establish their dominance on Student Council for the foreseeable future. It was also clear that this was the end of the road for the caucuses. It was a new world, and a new structure was needed to act as a counterpoint to the VPP. My particular concern was that the weakness of the caucuses would eventually carry over to the College officer elections, endangering the Honor System. So immediately after the election, I began having discussions with colleagues as to the future of the caucuses—conversations that would bear fruit the following fall.

Personally, I was not troubled by losing the election—I had anticipated that result going in. But I was very concerned about how the landscape had changed on Grounds, especially how things had become so political and personal. For the first time, I was made aware of the concept that if you don't agree with me, you're not a good person. This was the detritus of agenda-based politics at UVA, which was just rearing its ugly head, which would carry on through much of the 1970s, and which would reemerge in the current political landscape. It was highlighted and epitomized in the just-concluded election by the infamous "blue sheet" incident.

A few days prior to the election, Jack Rhodes, a traditional student leader, had authored a statement in support of the caucus candidates in response to a stream of negative press aimed at those candidates. This one-pager subsequently became known as the "white sheet." The white sheet was distributed around Grounds with an accompanying endorsement from many of the traditional student leaders. It was critical of the VPP but did not single out any of the VPP candidates or mention them by name; rather it emphasized the attributes of the caucus candidates and called for constructive, measured change. Well, that apparently stuck in the craw of the VPP, and the day before the election they issued a one-pager on blue paper (the "blue sheet") authored by one of the coalition and VPP founders. It was a nasty piece of work. All is fair and all that, but this flyer upped the ante on the smear letter of the previous fall and broke long-standing precedent by personally attacking a number of the caucus candidates (including yours truly) and using quite ungentlemanly language in the process. I distinctly remember someone handing me a copy of it while I was on my way to class and asking whether I had seen it. My first emotion was astonishment, which quickly yielded to outrage. Personal attacks against fellow students just weren't part of the UVA culture. Moreover, and what really shocked me, was the fact that the VPP hierarchy was chock full of my own fraternity brothers.

After class, and with a blue sheet in hand, I marched up to Alderman Road where Bruce Wine, VPP president and AEPi classmate, resided as a senior counselor. Even at that point, in my pollyannaish state, I couldn't believe that my fraternity brother and friend of the past three years would have authorized the issuance of such trash. When I arrived at his suite, I found Bruce surrounded by a group of VPP honchos gearing up for the election. Before I even asked the question, I knew the answer by the look on his face when he saw me. But I asked the question anyway: "Did you know this was going out before it was distributed?"

The answer was a one word "yes"—and with that I did an about-face and left the room. That was the last time I spoke to Bruce for twenty-five years—which was facilitated by the fact that he had pretty much abandoned his association with AEPi by then, and rarely if ever was seen at the house after that.[50]

The release of the blue sheet was met by a groundswell of criticism, and the next day the VPP issued an official apology in *The Cavalier Daily*. Claiming that the blue sheet was distributed only after the white sheet had come out, the VPP stated, "In his desire to set the record straight, Mr. Schenkkan committed the same error of generalization and smear attack of which he accused Mr. Rhoades [sic]. The VPP officially apologizes for the slander and sincerely wishes it to be known that whatever a man's political beliefs, we will never question his character, motives, or his honest desire to do what he feels is best for the

---

50    I finally reconciled with Bruce at our twenty-fifth reunion in 1995, when we both served on a panel with Edgar Shannon discussing the days of turmoil at UVA. I was pleased that occurred, as Bruce became fatally ill not long afterwards.

University… We apologize to Mr. Gardner and Mr. Martin and bid them think no less of our party for this incident."

It was an appropriate apology, but there was no real moral equivalence here as the white sheet had not attacked any VPP candidate individually or used derogatory language. And it was too little too late. But more importantly, the proverbial genie was out of the bottle. While this represented the first time that ad hominem attacks would be seen on Grounds, it would not be the last.

As for me, I was greatly disappointed and disillusioned. In my own little bubble, I believed that friendship trumped politics and that there was an overriding social compact on Grounds that subordinated causes to collegiality. In my mind, this was what set UVA apart from the strife and turmoil that had engulfed Cornell, Harvard, Columbia and so many other campuses across the country. But this little incident was a harbinger of things to come at UVA as my third year came to an end. Similar to the climate we live in today, those who challenged the "right" way of thinking or acting would be demonized, and contentiousness would subsume civility. Soon enough, causes and politics would become ascendant, and the culture and mores of the Old U would slip into the mists of the past.

# —FOURTH YEAR—
## REVOLUTION
*1969-1970*

# Introduction

Ah, the summer of 1969. One of the most momentous summers in recent American history. The moon landing on July 20 was one of the signal events of the twentieth century. I think every person of my generation remembers where they were the moment Neil Armstrong first set foot on the moon. Of course, I was back at camp carousing with my friends and trying to stay out of trouble. But at that moment, everything came to a halt and we all gathered around a commandeered TV to watch the historic event. Even more so in retrospect, the achievement of that goal was astonishing. I was in third grade in October 1957, when Russia announced that it had launched Sputnik, the first space satellite, shocking America and triggering the great space race. Yet less than twelve years later, the U.S. had put a man on the moon. It was an accomplishment arguably unparalleled in the history of mankind and demonstrated in Jeffersonian terms what the illimitable freedom of the human mind could achieve. It was also the summer of Chappaquiddick, which effectively ended the possibility of another Kennedy presidency, and the summer of the Stonewall riots in New York City, which marked the beginning of the gay rights movement. But even with all this happening, for my generation, the summer of 1969 will probably most be remembered as the summer of Woodstock.

The Woodstock music festival took place in Bethel, New York, over four days in August 1969. With over four hundred thousand people attending and an unparalleled gathering of the greatest icons of the music world performing (the Grateful Dead; Janis Joplin; Jimi Hendrix; the Who; Crosby, Stills, Nash & Young, etc.), this event marked the pinnacle of the counterculture generation. The world watched as in the fields and mud of Yasgur's farm any sense of reserve left from the America of the 1950s disappeared. It was drugs, sex, and music with little else on the agenda.

171

While I didn't attend the festivities, our camp was less than thirty miles from the festival and the mood of Woodstock was very much upon us. It was a wild summer, and it did not take a genius to figure out that profound changes were occurring in America and that UVA would not be immune to these. So I headed back to Charlottesville feeling that my fourth year could well contain some very new and different experiences.

One thing I was sure of was that my final year as an undergraduate would be a very busy one. Firstly, the proverbial chickens of the honors program would be coming home to roost. While most of my classmates would inevitably be slowing down academically and ramping up socially in preparation for graduation, I had to formulate, research, and write my honors thesis as well as prepare for my honors oral and written exams. In addition, I was loaded with extracurricular activities, including being Master (president) of AEPi, serving on the IFC Rush Board, and writing my column for the *CD*. Furthermore, I was intent on following up on the initial discussions held in the spring about what to do with the moribund fraternity caucuses.

Shortly after decamping on Grounds, I experienced the greatest honor of my collegiate career, and a most unexpected one at that—I was inducted into the Z Society. Thus began a relationship with the most outstanding group of individuals I have had the fortune to know then and since. And as the year progressed, I was totally humbled by an increasing number of honors—Phi Beta Kappa, T.I.L.K.A, Raven Society, ODK National Leadership Fraternity. I never imagined three short years earlier when I first set foot on Grounds that any of this would be possible for this stranger in a strange land. But first things first, as I had plenty on my plate as I moved into the Crackerbox.

## *The Crackerbox*

Toward the end of the prior spring semester, I had submitted my application to live on the Lawn. This was and still is a very competitive process and is considered a great honor for a Wahoo. One may ask why so many students want to live in these tiny, approximately twelve-by-thirteen-foot cubicles, with no indoor plumbing other than a sink, no air conditioning, and a long outdoor jaunt to a shower or toilet. Well, at an institution that has long honored tradition, living in the midst of Mr. Jefferson's original Academical Village is arguably the most traditional path one can take. For those living on the Lawn, there is an unmistakable bond with those past Wahoos who have stoked the fire in the same ancient fireplace, who have sat in the same rocking chair watching their fellow students, professors, and tourists parade by and who have strolled in their bathrobes along the same colonnades and down the same alleys to take a shower.[51] In any event, numerous rising fourth-years want to live on the Lawn, and I was fortunate to be selected to do so.

*The Crackerbox in 1969—little has changed*

Prior to actual room selection, my buddy Steve Hayes, who had also been honored with a Lawn room, approached me and asked whether I would like to join him in living in the Crackerbox. Like many, if not most, UVA students, I had heard the name but really didn't know much about it. The Crackerbox is a two-story brick structure located

---

51  In each Lawn room is a plaque listing chronologically each prior resident of that room.

between the back of the lower garden of Pavilion X and the rear of Hotel F of the East Range. It was not part of Mr. Jefferson's original plan for the Academical Village and its origins are uncertain, although it is generally believed to be circa 1840s (I have seen a print of the University dated 1856 where the Crackerbox is prominently displayed therein). The original purpose of the building is lost in the shrouds of history. Various theories include it being a kitchen, a smokehouse, slave quarters, or even a bordello. No matter, as of 1969 it was the smallest "dorm" on Grounds and considered to be part of the Lawn for residency purposes.[52]

The benefits of living in the Crackerbox were threefold. First and foremost, there was a lavatory and shower in the basement of Hotel F, which was mere steps from the Crackerbox, thus making it the shortest trip to the head of any residence on the Lawn or Ranges. Second, you had the use of the lower garden of Pavilion X, which was directly outside the building and up a few steps. It was like having your own private backyard. And third, although only a two-minute walk up the serpentine wall-lined alley to the Lawn proper, it was an extremely quiet and serene location. Also, as a bonus, the Crackerbox contained the largest fireplace of any building in the Academical Village. And personally, there was an added benefit in that the Crackerbox is only steps from Randall Hall, which at that time was the home of the history department, where I would be spending a fair amount of time in my fourth year.

So Hayes and I decided to room in the Crackerbox, and it was everything as advertised. On a freezing winter morning, it was an easy stroll to the shower, and on a beautiful fall or spring afternoon, I would do my studying on a bench in the verdant solitude of Pavilion X's lower garden. But most of all, it was living in the splendor of Mr. Jefferson's creation that I will never forget. It was a transporting experience that helped make my final undergraduate year at UVA such a special one.

---

52   At some point, the Crackerbox became part of the Range residences and therefore reserved for graduate students.

## *Counterculture Meets Cavalier Culture*

Once back in Cville, it did not take long to see the impact of Woodstock Nation on life at UVA. First was the noticeable decrease in the number of coats and ties on Grounds. While there had been a slow but steady erosion of this tradition over the prior two years, there was now visible a marked acceleration of this trend. Whereas about ninety-five percent wore a coat and tie daily when I arrived in 1966, that number was probably less than fifty percent by the fall of 1969. Blazers, cuffed khakis and club ties were being replaced by bell bottom jeans and work shirts. Furthermore, hair length was substantially longer and facial hair had probably made its most widespread appearance on Grounds since the nineteenth century.

In addition to the observable stylistic changes rendered by the growth of the counterculture movement, perhaps a more significant occurrence was the blossoming of the drug culture. Drug use had been slowly but surely gaining traction at UVA since my second year. In fact, it had become enough of an issue that in the summer of 1968, the new Dean of Students, Alan Williams, sent out a letter stating that UVA students found using or otherwise involved with drugs may be subject to suspension. Indeed, incoming students in September of 1969 were greeted with a front-page article in *The Cavalier Daily* entitled "Drugs Flow at UVA Despite Legal Penalties," which noted, "Although the names 'Rebel Yell,' 'Cutty Sark' and 'Black and White' are more familiar to University students than 'Acapulco Gold,' 'Deep Purple' or 'Black Beauties,' an increasing number of students are breaking away from the traditional alcoholic intoxicants in favor of more head-oriented drugs." And the *CD* was right on, as drug use truly became a widespread phenomenon my fourth year.

Suddenly more and more folks seemed to be smoking weed. These included many Old U types one wouldn't have thought would be indulging. And it was more than just marijuana—it was hash, opium, Quaaludes and, more profoundly, the psychedelic drugs such as mescaline, psilocybin, and LSD. Now don't get me wrong, not every Wahoo was getting high and it was a distinct minority who were tripping, but there was a material change in drug use that in its own way would have a real impact on student life at the University. You see, there was a big difference between the drinking culture and drug culture at UVA. As noted earlier, drinking was a social activity. It mostly took place at parties or during a group activity like going down the road. Outside of a beer here and there, there was very little drinking during the week or by oneself. For various reasons, including the glaring fact that it was illegal, drug use usually took place behind closed doors and in smaller intimate groups. One tended not to light up at a party, in the living room of the fraternity house or while grabbing a burger at The Virginian. This led to more students hanging out in apartments and in small groups rather than at frat houses or at parties. Furthermore, there was a lot more toking than chugging taking place during the week and on non-party weekends. I did not know any alcoholics during my time at UVA, but I did have friends and acquaintances who became addicted to drugs in a relatively short time frame. Some of them never really recovered, and things did not end well for a few. Thus, for several reasons, I viewed the rise of the drug culture as a far greater negative for life on Grounds than drinking had ever been—just one person's view.

~~~~~

The rise of the counterculture at UVA was by no means a tsunami, and there still remained quite a strong Old U contingent. The growing divide was tangible. As history has shown, a culture threatened is a culture aroused. And it was no different at UVA, where a vigorous backlash to the many changes arose. This was best expressed in a phrase that became popular at the time—"Bring Back the Old U" or "BBTOU" for short. BBTOU buttons suddenly appeared for sale on the Corner and were proudly worn on many a blazer. But in a way, it was very much like the Gone with the Wind analogy I referenced in the Introduction. It was a longing for a disappearing lifestyle that was simpler and more collegial; where politics and causes took a backseat to camaraderie and sociability. But, as we shall see, this too was a lost cause, as the divide would only get wider as the school year progressed.

## The War Takes Center Stage

The big news on Grounds at the beginning of the fall semester were carryovers from the prior school year—the imminence of coeducation and progress in the efforts to attain de facto integration. The major headline the first week of classes involved a federal court injunction forcing the admittance of coeds into the College of Arts & Sciences in Charlottesville. In the spring of 1969, four plaintiffs had filed a complaint against the University claiming they had been denied admission to UVA on the basis of sex. As it turned out, only one of the four women would actually enroll in the fall of 1969 on the basis of Judge Mehrige's injunction—thus making Virginia Ann Scott the first female student admitted to the College. While this was a historic moment, the decision had already in effect been made to admit women as of the fall of 1970, and a few months later the court would in effect uphold the Board of Visitors' plan for coeducation.

The other big story was the appointment of Virginia Johnson as Assistant Dean of Admissions, becoming the first full-time black admissions officer. Shortly thereafter, the administration also announced the creation of a faculty committee for black studies. Thus President Shannon seemed to be following through on his promises to take civil rights issues seriously. Accordingly, with the civil rights and coeducation issues apparently being effectively addressed, the activists on Grounds turned their attention to another major issue raging across America, one which had essentially lain dormant at UVA the prior school year—the Vietnam War.

After the first few weeks of classes, we were greeted on a Monday morning with a headline blazoned across the front page of the *CD* reading, "The Vietnam War must end now." It announced a call by a new group named the Vietnam Moratorium Committee for anti-war activities to take place on campuses across the country. The centerpiece of the committee's plan was for a nationwide "moratorium" to take place on October 15, which would entail a one-day halt to all research and classroom activities. According to the organizers, the day instead was to be spent working against the war by demonstrating, distributing leaflets and petitions, etc. The *CD* noted that the committee's leaders had chosen the term "moratorium" to describe the interruption of classes rather than "strike," because they considered the latter term too inflammatory. But in reality, they were calling for a student and faculty strike on all college campuses.

Well, it did not take long for the UVA Vietnam Moratorium Committee and its Student Council supporters to roll into action. The Student Council passed a resolution calling for a meeting between Council President Bud Ogle and President Shannon to discuss the cancellation of classes on October 15. President Shannon, in his typical understated and diplomatic style, responded that he would give the request "the most serious consideration." Meanwhile, the UVA faculty became involved in the controversy to a degree lacking in the protests and activities of the prior school year. A number of faculty members openly supported the moratorium, led by Professor John Israel of the history department. At the same time, other members of the faculty vocally opposed the moratorium or strike or whatever moniker you put on it—"a rose by any other name…" Professor Inis Claude Jr. of the government department had this to say: "The University is an institution of learning, properly dedicated to the promotion of studying and teaching. It should not be available for use by anybody or by everybody as an ideological base or political instrument." Wise words as true now as then, for one never knows when the proverbial worm will turn.

In any event, not surprisingly, President Shannon closed the door on shutting down classes. He issued a statement asserting, "The University has an obligation to maintain an atmosphere in which all views can be expressed, in which individuals can oppose the war or defend it, or advocate various means of ending it, as a matter of academic and intellectual freedom." However, the administration's decision to keep the

University open for business did not deter the Moratorium Committee from planning a day full of anti-war events, including demonstrations, marches, and a concert of protest to top off the activities.

I remember October 15, 1969, well. An estimated fifteen hundred people attended a noontime rally on the north side of the Rotunda in support of the moratorium, marking the first major anti-war protest at the University. But what I recall most about that day is that two of my fraternity brothers were involved in incidents that made the front page of *The Cavalier Daily* the following day. As part of the day's activities, there was a peace march that traversed most areas of the University. Included in the march was a "peace wagon" pulled by a tractor. As the march proceeded up Rugby Road, my fraternity brother Jeff "Zippy" Lorber, who was marching alongside the tractor, was distracted and was struck by the tractor, which rolled over his foot and dragged him under. Fortunately for Zip, someone quickly pulled him out just as the rear wheels were about to run over his body, which would have had tragic consequences. I remember Jeff being on crutches for many weeks after the march—his protestor's "purple heart."

The other AEPi-related incident involved Jeff Kirsch, a third-year Pi man and an activist leader. As the rally at the Rotunda was about to begin, Jeff attempted to lower to half-mast the U.S. flag in front of the Rotunda. Immediately, another student raised it back to full-mast, at which point Jeff approached Dean Alan Williams and requested that he be allowed to lower the flag again—to which Dean Williams pithily replied, "Not a chance."

So UVA weathered its first major anti-war protest; but it did not go down without incident. A serious confrontation occurred during the march—the first time in my experience at UVA, and perhaps in decades, that groups of UVA students almost came to blows over something other than whiskey and women. As the "peace" march went by the Alderman Road and Observatory Hill dorms, the marchers began to sing "We Shall Overcome," and one of the leaders of the march approached the dorms and asked the many students who were lining the balconies to join the march. This was met by groups of students shouting "win the war" as they went down to the street to continue the verbal jousting. With the chants of "win the war" opposing the verses of "We Shall Overcome," the two groups confronted one another. A counselor from Watson dorm was later quoted as saying, "I looked down from the dormitory and realized that a dangerous confrontation was in the offing. There was only about ten feet separating the two groups." Fortunately, cooler heads prevailed and the marchers moved on before anything more than sequential shouting could take place.

Thus in the fall of 1969, politics had finally become ascendant, rupturing the social bond that for decades had united most Wahoos. I witnessed this very directly in the AEPi house, where the fraternity effectively, if not formally, broke into two camps—the "peace and love" group and the "good old boys." I leave it to your imagination which group I gravitated towards. However, as Master of the house (not in the Les Miserables sense), I felt it was my responsibility to try to bring as many guys together on as many levels as possible. I had dear friends in both factions and I hated to see bonds of friendship weakened or torn apart by politics. At the end of the day we kept most of the house together, but we did lose a few fellows who just couldn't conflate the concept of being a fraternity member with their self-image as activists.

The reality was that the anti-war issue had proved to be much more divisive than the Student Coalition-led activities of the year before. In retrospect, I believe that was because most UVA students believed in the ultimate goal of the coalition—the end of racial discrimination at UVA—while disagreeing mainly on methods to achieve that goal. On the other hand, the anti-war movement's goal—the immediate end of the war and evacuation of American troops—was strongly opposed at that time by both a large contingent of UVA students and the American public at large. Moreover, certain elements of the anti-war movement exacerbated matters by provocative actions such as waving Viet Cong flags and hoisting pictures of Ho Chi Minh at the same time these enemies were killing our friends, relatives, and countrymen. There was no doubt that emotions ran high on both sides.

Tensions at the University were further raised by some very un-UVA-like behavior displayed by certain leaders of the anti-war contingent. A prime example of this came during a speech sponsored by the Law School's Student Legal Forum (SLF). The SLF, founded in the 1940s, had a celebrated history of bringing famous and consequential political, governmental and legal speakers to UVA. Past heads of the SLF included both Robert and Ted Kennedy. In December, the SLF invited Deputy Attorney General Richard Kleindienst to speak at the University. Well, Richard Nixon's Justice Department under Attorney General John Mitchell was particularly reviled by anti-war activists. So it was expected that there might be some demonstrations outside the auditorium and that some pointed questions might be directed to Mr. Kleindienst. What was not expected was that the guest speaker would be repeatedly heckled and interrupted during his speech, actions that pushed the protest envelope that much further.

The prior spring, most folks on Grounds had been shocked when protesters had silently stood up and walked out of President Shannon's presentation during the Sesquicentennial celebrations. Actively and vocally disrupting a speech was a new and extraordinary form of protest that engendered strong negative reactions. The SLF severely criticized the hecklers in an open letter to the University. Expressing its "abhorrence" for the disruptive behavior, it excoriated the "irrational and immature conduct" and "McCarthy era tactics" utilized, and finally noted that such actions could very well impinge on its ability to bring other speakers to UVA. This behavior was even too much for *The Cavalier Daily*, which had been a major moratorium supporter. In an editorial entitled "Childish Arrogance," the editors asserted, "We have no quarrel with those who despise what Richard Kleindienst stands for. But when they use such tactics as witnessed Thursday night, we come to a parting of the ways. The methods are not only wrong but counterproductive." In my mind, the *CD* was being a bit disingenuous. You can't despise and demonize people and groups, which the *CD* was increasingly apt to do, without expecting this type of behavior.

In the end, the growing intensity of the anti-war movement resulted in serious divisions at UVA. Feelings were rising ever higher, and this would lay the groundwork for the events to come at the end of the following semester. Furthermore, the burgeoning web of the counter-culture/anti-war ethos was expanding to ensnare other totems of the establishment and status quo. The usual suspects called for ROTC to be removed from Grounds, opposed certain corporations peripherally involved in the war being allowed to recruit at UVA, and even challenged having a graduate business school at the University. Not surprisingly, the newly formed Radical Student Union, a successor organization to various radical groups, would deliver a harsh attack on the Honor System, calling it "farcical" and one of the "great irrelevancies" in the pursuit of knowledge. And to further fan the flames of divisiveness on Grounds, the *CD* would unleash an unprecedented frontal assault on that old bugaboo of the social left—the fraternity system.

## *What Are You Afraid Of?*

As an imperfect institution in an imperfect world, and as a perceived pillar of the Old U, the fraternity system and its members had been the subject of increasing attacks over the past few semesters. But nothing seen previously could be compared to the infamous vituperative *Cavalier Daily* editorial "On Rush," which ended with the admonition "Don't rush, Don't pledge." The editorial was chock full of insulting goodies. The fraternity system was admonished as "a slowly dying anachronism" defined by "narrow-minded bigotry" unchanged from when it was founded to foster "the elitist concept of the racist Southern gentleman." New pledges were expected to be "the type of person that the members don't generally have the initiative to make of themselves."

Well, so much for civil discourse. Since about forty-five percent of UVA undergraduates were fraternity members, this was a hell of an indictment of a substantial part of the student body. Not that the fraternity system was above criticism, because like most institutions—particularly social institutions—the organizations reflected the weak-

nesses and frailties of its members. There were plenty of issues surrounding fraternities to be discussed rationally and intelligently. But
this invective was full of so much name-calling and so many gross
generalizations, exaggerations, and outright fictions that it took rational discussion off the table and drove a noxious wedge between major
elements of the student body.

Needless to say, this editorial certainly stirred the proverbial pot,
and reaction was quick and plentiful. It was even too much for some
fellow members of the *CD*'s Managing Board. Managing Editor Rod
McDonald responded the next day with a highly critical column point-
ing out the numerous fallacies in the arguments set forth in the editorial:

> First-year men this year are being told a variety of
> myths: that fraternities are fading out (when in fact
> they increase each year); that they beat their pledges;
> and that pledges exist solely for the use of sadistic
> brothers. These myths, hope the opponents, will con-
> vince an interested student to avoid pledging until
> after his first year, when it is generally too late. But the
> prevalent myth is that fraternity men are all Southern
> gentlemen, conservative bigots, narrow-minded and
> oppressive mentors of their fraternity brothers. Such an
> approach sadly neglects the facts. No two fraternities,
> and for that matter no two people, are exactly alike.
> Fraternities all have diverse viewpoints, and their shares
> of non-three-piece suit wardrobes, and the fraternity
> system has produced some of the more respected liberal
> politicians in the student body—Paul Hurdle, Steve
> Hayes and Kevin Mannix, for examples.

Perhaps the best response to "Don't rush, Don't pledge" came from
Bob Fisher, the President of the IFC. Bob was extremely bright (Phi
Beta Kappa), very measured, and a student leader all the way. In a let-

ter to the editor, he took to task the prejudices and closed-mindedness displayed in the editorial. First noting that he had a difficult time being neutral because of his own positive experiences with the fraternity system, he then dealt with many of the allegations set forth in the editorial and wondered why there were no constructive suggestions offered, only attacks. He closed brilliantly as follows:

> I would question your motives and your fears: 'Don't Rush, Don't Pledge.' What are you afraid of? First-year men today, more than ever before, are endowed with an intellectual inquisitiveness, as well as a sturdy measure of critical judgement. You advise them to waste these capabilities, to hold the 'prejudices' which you personally hold, and to commit the 'unforgivable sin' of bearing a closed mind which you accuse people in fraternities of bearing. In this sense I believe you have compromised any confidence which the first-year men might have in your reasoning.

And so the rising tide of activism and counter-culturalism continued to set Wahoos against each other—anti-war versus pro-war; radicals versus traditionalists; fraternity men versus independents. What had once been an amazingly unified student body was now suffering the same divisions that had rent asunder many other college campuses across the nation.

## The Birth of the Jefferson Party

As the tumult grew at the beginning of fall semester, I became more convinced that the timing was now or never to hasten the demise of the fraternity caucuses and create a new entity as a counterbalance to the VPP. I noted previously that I had been involved in discussions in that regard the prior spring after Student Council elections. Shortly after classes started in September, a student study committee was created to examine the activities and future of the caucuses. I participated in the study group, which ultimately determined that the caucuses were not fulfilling a realistic political function on Grounds, that they represented only a select group of students, and that they were no longer electing candidates on a regular basis. It was also decided that a new entity was needed that would be open to all students on a democratic basis and that would appeal not only to a wide base of fraternity members, but also to independents and first-year students, who had not previously been represented at the caucuses. And thus the Jefferson Party (JP) was born—and I was honored to be elected its first president. The two caucuses were dissolved a few weeks later.

In my mind, the ultimate goal of the JP was to preserve and protect those attributes of the University that defined "UVA exceptionalism"—those values that made the UVA experience such a unique and special one. First and foremost was the Honor System. And close behind was the Wahoo social compact of civility and camaraderie, sprinkled with the Jeffersonian belief in individual freedom and responsibility—in essence the time-honored concept in Charlottesville that there was mutual respect among students for doing whatever one wanted outside the classroom as long as one didn't hurt anyone else. This led to a community of collegiality and cohesiveness. If a student wanted to spend his time singing "Kumbaya" and going on peace marches, that was fine; if he wanted to spend his time hanging with his fraternity brothers and going down the road, that was fine; if he wanted to spend his time "hawking"[53] in Alderman Library or being a "politico," that was fine; and if he wanted to march up and down the Grounds in a uniform and interview with Dow Chemical, that was fine, too. To each his own— that was the Virginia way. But both the Honor System and the social compact were under unprecedented attack by forces that disdained any remnants of the Old U, were convinced of their own moral superiority, and thought that the University should be a means to achieve certain social or political agendas. Indeed, the atmosphere at UVA in 1969

---

53 "Studying" in common parlance.

was not unlike the atmosphere on many campuses across the country today, where the diversity of thought has been suborned to social agendas, where opposing points of view are deprecated, and where, in essence, it's "my way or the highway" rather than "live and let live."

So my colleagues and I set out to try to forge a coalition of students that would be supportive of the values noted above. I felt that a majority of students at the University at that time were still in agreement with those values—but many of these folks were among the most apathetic on Grounds, in effect, still living in the "bubble." Sort of UVA's version of the "silent majority." As a result, we cast our net wide and canvassed many different groups, clubs and societies that had never participated in the caucuses, or in any other University electoral group for that matter. In the end, we put together a fairly impressive initial group of active leaders and created a structure that encouraged group participation. When I now look at the Jefferson Party photo in the 1970 edition of the *Corks and Curls*, I can only smile when I see that the initial leadership of the JP included numerous individuals who would go on to serve the University well. There is Tom Faulders, past President of the UVA Alumni Association; Lee Garret, past Chair of the College's Benefactors Society; and Jim Gilmore, former Attorney General and Governor of the Commonwealth.

Shortly after the Jefferson Party was formed, the VPP instituted a number of changes patterned after what we had done with the JP, making the VPP more participatory. And the VPP elected a new president, Stu Pape, my classmate and fraternity brother. Thus, in the fall of 1969, the AEPi house sported the presidents of the two student political parties on Grounds. Having two Jewish fraternity boys from public high schools in New York and New Jersey as presidents of both the traditional and liberal parties pretty much put to rest the canard that the fraternity system was some sort of monolithic fortress of elitist Southern bigotry.

*Founding Fathers of the Jefferson Party*

As it turned out, the creation of the JP was a wise decision for many reasons. Along with the VPP, it opened up University student representation to many more people than had been involved previously. It also created an effective counterbalance to the VPP at a crucial period in the history of the University. It did not happen all at once, as predictably the VPP dominated the Student Council elections in the fall. But my eyes had always been on the Honor System and the College officer elections in the spring. And there, amidst some particularly vicious attacks launched against the system, the JP candidates for president and vice president, David Morris and David Bowman, surprised most everybody by winning overwhelming victories. Thus, in a period of turmoil and change, the "silent majority" of Wahoos made their voice heard in support of continuing a traditionalist approach to the crown jewel of the University's traditions. And for me, the frosting on the cake came shortly thereafter when the University held its first direct election for Student Council officers (previously, the officers were elected internally by the Student Council members). While VPP candidate and long-time council member Kevin Mannix ran unopposed for the presidency, JP candidate Hugh Antrim had the tough task of running against VPP candidate and also long-time council member Tony Sherman for the vice presidency. To everyone's amazement, including my own, Antrim won the election, thus ensuring a balanced leadership on Student Council—something that would be sorely needed just weeks afterwards.

## *A Barrier is Broken*

As of the fall of 1969, a black student had never been pledged by an established University fraternity. The prior year, a fraternity in the process of being "colonized" had taken a black student as a prospective member. But formal rush had never produced a black pledge in over a hundred years of fraternity life at UVA—a disgrace, but in reality not surprising given the University's civil rights history. Indeed, it would have been difficult to pledge black students when there were virtually none around. And, as we have seen, it was not until the spring of 1969 that UVA finally became committed to truly integrating the University. The fall rush of 1969 was the first since that had occurred—and so the time was propitious for history to be made.

As noted previously, I had been elected to serve on the IFC Rush Board for the fall of 1969. There was a fair amount of informal discussion going on in response to the racism charges directed at the fraternity system, but it soon became clear that no formal action or statement would be made by the IFC regarding rush. The issue would lie in the hands of each individual house.

At the time, as Master of AEPi, I knew this issue would be front and center at the house for fall rush. I had previously heard stories that we had come close to pledging one of the handful of black students during rush my first year in 1966. Apparently, at that point, there was a hardcore block of resistance that could not be breached, and that effort failed. In the prior two years, the issue had not arisen. For one reason or another, our fault or not, no black student had rushed the house. But now, that prior block of resistance was mostly gone, and as rush approached, the prevailing sentiment was that we should actively open rush to black students. Some wanted to do this to make a statement; others felt that since we were now rushing non-Jewish students as a matter of course, we should treat all first-years equally—a good guy was a good guy, no matter religion, race, etc. These feelings were representative of most of the brotherhood. But I knew where the potential problems rested and knew they had to be dealt with prior to the beginning of rush. Accordingly, a few well-placed and private discussions early in the semester defused what might have been significant problems later on.

Fall 1969 rush was probably the most open one ever for our chapter, and I am proud to say that we participated in making UVA history by pledging our first black student—James "Bubba" Small. As it turned out, a total of five black students were offered bids that fall, finally breaking the racial barrier and ending an unfortunate chapter in UVA history. It was hardly a cause for celebration, as it only marked a small step forward. But it was a step forward nonetheless, and one that would be built upon as time went on. Most fraternities would subsequently follow suit and open their doors to a broader segment of the student body and a number of black fraternities would also be established on Grounds.

As a generalization, the actions of UVA's fraternities would parallel the broader trends of the University's civil rights history—a backhanded compliment at best. As I put pen to paper, the undergraduate enrollment of black students at UVA as a percentage is about half of what it was twenty-five years ago.

## A Night to Remember

I am fairly certain that most Wahoos in my age group remember exactly where they were on the evening of December 1, 1969. Because it was on that date that the U.S. Selective Service System held its first draft lottery since 1942. You see, by December 1969, troop levels in Vietnam were still near their peak at over five hundred thousand, and since the interminable war seemed to have no end in sight, large numbers of young men were in demand to feed the war machine. Moreover, attacks on the draft had been escalating with growing claims that the war was mostly being fought by poor and working-class kids while the wealthy and privileged sat it out with real or manufactured deferments. Well, that was pretty much true; and President Nixon, wanting to protect his position with the "silent majority," decided to create an aura of fairness through a random selection lottery.

Thus, on December 1, a drawing was held at Selective Service national headquarters in Washington, D.C. that would determine the 1970 draft status of every man between the ages of eighteen to twenty-six. That night, Wahoos all over the Grounds congregated at various venues—apartments, dorms, frat houses, bars. Not surprisingly, I was ensconced at the Pi lodge with dozens of my fraters. Once again, the party room was set up theater style, with the TV center stage and rows of chairs lined up in front of it. A pool was created to be awarded to the brother with the lowest draft number, and the beer machine was quickly emptied as we took our seats and waited for the show to begin. And this was how the lottery was done: each day of the year was represented on a slip of paper and placed in a blue capsule, which was then placed in a large glass container and mixed around with all the other 365 capsules. The capsules would then be drawn by hand to assign order-of-call numbers, from lowest to highest.

Well, you can imagine the tension and anxiety in the room at the Pi house as Congressman Alexander Pirnie of the House Armed Services Committee dipped his hand into the container to begin picking the dates. We all knew that the course of the next few years of our lives could well be determined by the sequence number assigned to each of our birthdays. It did not take long for the winner of the AEPi pool to be determined, as one of the brothers was stunned by his birthday being the second capsule pulled. After that, we each held our breath as capsule after capsule was plucked from the container. I sat there on pins and needles as the numbers went by—50, 75, 100. When they reached 150 and my birthday had still not been called, I started to breathe a bit easier. It had not been specifically determined at that point where the safety zone was, although most agreed that one was probably safe at 200 or higher. After they reached 165, I remember getting up to get something to drink and suddenly heard my buddy Steve Hayes' birthday called. I was just saying to myself, "There goes Hayes," when my birthday was the very next one picked. And I immediately thought to myself, "High, but not high enough"—and as it turned out, I was absolutely correct.

So the evening ended with some of the guys with high numbers going out and partying, and others, such as myself, starting to think seriously about how to deal with a potential future in fatigues and khaki. I certainly did not intend to wait to be drafted after graduating, so I began to ponder proactive alternatives. Some fellows talked of going to Canada, some of entering the clergy, and some discovered newfound ailments that certain well-paid doctors were willing to affirm. But none of those were routes I was about to follow. Rather, I decided both to take the Officer Candidate School exam and to apply to several Army Reserve units and go with the first opportunity that arose. That turned out to be an Army Security Agency reserve unit, in which I enlisted that spring, thus assuring me a new and totally different life experience for the year after I graduated.

## *The Calm Before the Storm*

While the escalating anti-war fervor had dominated events during the fall semester, spring semester opened fairly quietly and pretty much continued that way through April. For me, the honors history chickens were roosting big time. I was spending most of my time in the bowels of Alderman Library researching and writing my honors thesis. Contemporaneously, most of my classmates were spending most of their time making nostalgic road trips and finding other entertaining ways to occupy their final few months in Charlottesville.

Much of the news on Grounds involved progress in implementing civil rights initiatives. The College announced that it was hiring its first two black faculty members and the faculty approved a major in Afro-American studies. There was at that point one black athlete on the first-year football team and two on the first-year basketball team, and the athletic department announced that four more black football players had been signed for the following year. In January, Jim Roebuck from Graduate Arts & Sciences had been elected the first black President of Student Council.

As for the anti-war movement, activities were on a fairly low flame. Much of the news in the spring involved the faculty fighting over whether to continue degree credit for ROTC courses. After an initial decision to disallow credit, some major backtracking occurred. With the faculty seemingly divided fifty-fifty on the issue, a compromise was eventually worked out. A new anti-war organization called Virginia Mobe (Mobilization to End the War in Vietnam), in addition to attacking ROTC, also condemned the existence of the JAG (Judge Advocates General's) School at UVA.

But these were low-level protests, and the whole atmosphere on Grounds was much calmer than it had been the previous semester. Of more interest to most students was the announcement of a major change in the academic schedule. Beginning in the 1971-1972 school year, exams would be scheduled before Christmas break and a twenty-six-day holiday would be instituted from mid-December to mid-January. Also, spring exams would take place in early May rather than early June. Thus would end the ridiculous situation where a truncated Christmas break was never really a holiday, with exams looming on the horizon.

Before we knew it, Easters Weekend was upon us, and it appeared to serve as a release from all the tension that had built up in the fall. The festivities began Thursday night, April 16, and included a bonfire in Mad Bowl that wound up consuming an old auto that had been rolled down the hill from Mad Lane. Sunday's grain parties in Mad Bowl would witness the beginning of an Easters tradition that would eventually contribute to the downfall of this weekend extravaganza.

With music blasting, the grain-laced purple passion flowing, and temperatures heating up, someone got a hose and started spraying down participants and then hosing down the east slopes of the bowl. Soon there was a torrent of mud along those slopes and scores of partygoers sliding down the slopes into the pool of mud below. Thus began the notorious Easters mudslides, which would grow in size and intensity as the years passed, would cause the infamous McCormick Road plumbing disaster and would provide fodder for those administrators looking for reasons to terminate these bacchanalian festivities.

With Easters Weekend over and only about a month left until exams, it seemed that the semester would end uneventfully. I had just about finished my thesis and would be submitting it at the beginning of May. I was also in the midst of deciding which law school I would attend. I was fortunate to have a choice among Columbia, Penn, and UVA, although I knew I would be training with Uncle Sam for most of the following academic year. In any event, I was looking forward to spending the remaining month prior to my written and oral exams participating in some of the last semester festivities that most of my compatriots had been enjoying for months.

And thus the headlines in the *CD* on April 21 did not particularly resonate with me. It was announced that William Kunstler, famous anti-war activist and counsel for the legendary Chicago Seven, would be speaking at UVA on May 6. The *CD* also noted that President Nixon had announced that another 150,000 troops would be pulled out of Vietnam, bringing the total reduction to 265,000 by the end of May. So I figured this would further defuse the anti-war agitation and that we would have a peaceful last month or so until graduation. Little did I know that our little world in Charlottesville was about to undergo a tectonic shift unparalleled before or since in the history of the University—and that Mr. Kunstler would play a major role in it.

## *The Fuse Is Lit*

It happened all at once. One minute we were sitting around looking forward to class parties and pre-graduation festivities, and a few days later there were marches, demonstrations, and clarion calls for boycotts and strikes. Apparently, spring semester had in reality been a tinderbox waiting for the right spark. And that spark turned out to be President Nixon's announcement on the evening of Thursday, April 30, 1970, that he had committed several thousand U.S. combat troops to enter Cambodia and attack Communist-held positions along the border of South Vietnam. No matter that this was by no means a broad-based "invasion," but a geographically targeted incursion to disrupt a constant flow of troops and arms coming from North Vietnam through Cambodia into South Vietnam. It did represent an escalation in what had been a deescalating conflict—and it was enough to reignite the anti-war flames.

The reaction at UVA and most other colleges across the country was immediate. The Virginia Strike Committee was quickly established over the weekend. Most of its leaders were recognizable from their active participation in the moratorium movement the prior fall— Bud Ogle, Tom Gardner, Bruce Wine, and Jim Roebuck, amongst others. The Strike Committee called for a University-wide shutdown on Wednesday and Thursday, May 6 and 7, to "publicly express our protest on these issues (Cambodia, Vietnam, John Mitchell, Spiro Agnew, repression of Black Panthers and political dissent); support U.S. senate action against the war; analyze causes of domestic and international exploitation; and plan and take local and national action on the Indochina war, militarism, repression, ROTC, and University complicity." That was quite a mouthful. Anyway, in sympathy with the Strike Committee, a number of student leaders endorsed a boycott of classes on Wednesday and encouraged students to participate in "Freedom Day" activities scheduled for that day. Freedom Day activities would include "action sessions" and a free rock concert, and were to culminate with Bill Kunstler and late-entry "Yippie" leader and Chicago Seven icon Jerry Rubin speaking at University Hall. It seemed to me to be pretty much a repeat of the fall moratorium protests—and it probably would have been, except that all hell was about to break loose on that Monday.

I remember Monday, May 4, very well, as it was the day I handed in my honors thesis. As one can imagine, I was quite relieved to have that burden off my back. I was also quite interested in seeing how the new round of protests would play out. I now had some skin in the game, knowing that I would be going off to active duty in a few months. Even though I would be in the reserves, these units were still being activated on a regular basis. And while I wasn't ready to join the anti-war crowd yet, like most everyone my age who could not remember a time when the war was not going on, an early conclusion of the hostilities was greatly desired.

It was early afternoon when rumors started drifting in that something terrible had happened on the Kent State campus (in the pre-internet/iPhone era, news traveled rather slowly). By early evening, the news had circulated like wildfire. Four students had been killed and others wounded when a poorly trained and poorly led group of Ohio National Guardsmen had opened fire on a large crowd of Kent State students who had refused to disperse following days of demonstrations. The National Guard had been called in two days earlier, after protesters had set the university's ROTC building on fire and staged several violent demonstrations. There was little doubt that the guardsmen had been provoked that afternoon, with many of the demonstrators throwing rocks and other objects at them. But the guardsmen, many of whom were no older than the students they were facing, overreacted and fired indiscriminately into the crowd. Two of the students killed had not even been part of the demonstrations but were merely walking from one class to the next.

The news of the Kent State shootings fanned the flames of student discontent and turned the anti-war protests into a juggernaut that swept the Grounds. That evening, an estimated fifteen hundred students spontaneously converged on the Rotunda to condemn the shootings. After about a half-hour rally, the group marched the short distance to Carr's Hill, the home of the President of the University, to confront President Shannon. As the marchers approached Carr's Hill, President Shannon met them on the front porch. The leader of the march, Mark Krebs, was about as unlikely an agitator as one could imagine. From Birmingham, Alabama, Mark was a SAE, as Southern and traditional a fraternity as one could find at UVA. Mark had lived across the corridor from me in Humphreys first year, and the fact that he was now leading a demonstration marching on Carr's Hill was a concept that boggled my mind. Krebs read to President Shannon a proposed telegram to be sent to President Nixon condemning the escalation of the war and denouncing the shootings at Kent State, and then requested that Shannon sign it. While President Shannon would not agree to sign the telegram, he conveyed his appreciation for the students coming and presenting their "grave and deep concern." He was then asked to address a rally at 11 a.m. the next day but responded by saying he would not make a decision until the morning. Having delivered the message to President Shannon, many in the crowd dispersed, but one group broke off and marched across the Grounds to take the first in a series of actions that would escalate the protests to an unprecedented level at UVA.

After leaving Carr's Hill, a group of approximately sixty students gathered first in front of the Rotunda, blocking traffic, and then set off for Maury Hall, the demonstrators' initial target that evening. Maury Hall, a lesser-known building at the University located just southwest of McIntire Amphitheatre, also happened to be the home of the Navy ROTC program since its opening in 1942.

Meanwhile, several elected student leaders had been alerted to the gathering at Carr's Hill and the group's movement toward the Navy ROTC headquarters. So when the protesters reached Maury Hall, they were met by a small group of students, including David Morris and

David Bowman, the newly elected President and Vice-President of the College. After an initial confrontation between the groups, the protesters entered the building after protest leader Tom Gardner guaranteed that the sit-in could be monitored by student leaders. At the same time, additional interested students began to descend on Maury Hall. Some came in support of the protesters. But about fifty YAF[54] and ROTC members also entered the building, had a shouting match with the gathered protesters and proceeded to block the stairway leading upstairs where the arms and ammunition were stored. By early morning, there were approximately two hundred students of various persuasions occupying Maury Hall.

While all this was going on, the University's top administrators gathered in Pavilion V to develop a plan to deal with the budding crisis. It is important to remember that the Kent State debacle had flowed in great part from the torching of the ROTC building on that campus. Not long afterwards, the powers-that-be assembled in Pavilion V decided to get a court-ordered injunction enjoining the students from occupying Maury Hall or otherwise disrupting normal University activities. In reality, President Shannon had little other choice, apparently acting under an ultimatum from newly elected Governor Linwood Holton, the first Republican governor in Virginia since Reconstruction. As *The Cavalier Daily* editorial staff so aptly stated, "President Shannon had to face the political realities. As much as we like to think of the University as a bastion of academic freedom in a state not known for its tolerance, President Shannon was quite aware that he had very little time in which to take action before control passed out of his hands." Thus, at 4:20 a.m. Tuesday morning, Dean Alan Williams and Assistant Dean Robert Canevari went to Maury Hall and informed the occupying protesters that an injunction was to be delivered at any moment and described to them the consequences of not complying with the court order. Shortly before 5 a.m., the injunction was duly delivered and read to the jeering crowd by court officers. In consequence, the protesters

---

54  Young Americans for Freedom, a national conservative student organization.

promptly abandoned Maury Hall. Some of the group dispersed, but about half of them marched past the then-empty Pavilion V and made a return visit to Carr's Hill, where they were met by the president's wife, who asked them to leave. While some of the crowd began to taunt Mrs. Shannon, the assembled protesters dispersed shortly thereafter. And thus ended one of the most tumultuous days in UVA history—and little did anyone realize that this was to be only the tip of the iceberg.

Meanwhile, I was only a stone's throw from the excitement at Maury Hall, safely ensconced in the Crackerbox; and, like most of my fellow students, did not learn until the following day what had occurred the night before. The story of the Maury Hall takeover and the injunction quickly spread across Grounds as hundreds of students and faculty assembled at Old Cabell Hall for a noon memorial service for the Kent State students called by President Shannon and Student Council President Jim Roebuck. It was a short walk from the Crackerbox to Cabell Hall, and as I emerged on the Lawn, I could see there were dozens of Strike Committee supporters handing out black armbands and provocative literature. I took one of the armbands and politely declined the literature. At this point, in my mind it didn't matter whether you thought the war was immoral and illegal or an unfortunate necessity to stop the spread of Communism in Southeast Asia, or whether the incursion in Cambodia was an "expansion" of the war or a strategic move that would shorten the war in the long run. Our country had now reached the point where innocent kids on campus were being killed by ill-trained and frightened kids in uniform. So I put on the armband to mourn for the slain students as well as for those who had pulled the triggers. It was now a perilous period in our history, and for me what was important was to make sure that this evil of violence did not spread to Mr. Jefferson's village.

Cabell Hall was packed for the memorial service, and what I remember most about that event was how emotional and sincere President Shannon was in trying to both be empathetic to student concerns and preserve peace on Grounds. His voice cracking more than once while occasionally being jeered by the more radical members of the audience, Mr. Shannon expressed his grief for the deaths at Kent State during this "dark and divided time," but also emphasized the need for non-violence. Probably most importantly, he affirmed that the University must "remain a place to discuss our own views as to how to achieve peace. The University can't be an instrument of political purpose, for that would destroy the University and it could be overwhelmed by other pressures." Following President Shannon's speech, Jim Roebuck addressed the auditorium, and then the crowd filed out of the hall. The rest of the day was filled with members of the Strike Committee "rallying the troops" for the official boycott to begin the next day. Alexander Sedgwick of the history department announced during the day that while classes were not to be officially canceled on Wednesday, many teachers would not be holding them.

That evening, the Strike Committee, supported by a deeply divided Student Council, ramped up and extended the scope of the protests by presenting a list of nine "'demands" to President Shannon on the steps of Alderman Library. These included the immediate revocation of the court injunction, the complete removal of ROTC from the University, the severing of UVA's relationship with the JAG school, the termination of all research relationships with the defense department, support for University employees' right to strike and a commitment to a twenty percent goal for black admissions.

Clearly the demands went well beyond ending the war and bringing the boys home. And it did not take a Nostradamus to divine that few if any of these demands would be accepted. The strike leaders had unquestionably lost focus, and there were serious divisions among the University community regarding support for these demands. This was evident in the Student Council vote in support of the demands, which was 11 in favor, 10 against, and 1 abstention. Similarly, pro-strike faculty member Bill Harbaugh commented that hasty action on the demands would cause the faculty to revolt. So with the list of demands in hand, President Shannon headed back to Carr's Hill. This marked the termination of Tuesday's activities—a somewhat less eventful day than Monday, but one that set the stage for the first official day of the strike on Wednesday.

Wednesday, May 6, was a beautiful spring day in Charlottesville. The balmy weather and the fact that many classes were cancelled or made optional led to the largest student turnout yet for the "Freedom Day" events. The throngs of students were supplemented by a growing number of outsiders attracted to the protest activities and particularly to the much-awaited appearances that evening of Bill Kunstler and Jerry Rubin. In this heady mix of national conflict, demonstrations and outside agitation, the potential for violence was ever present. This was recognized by the constant pleas for restraint and peaceful protest by various student leaders, faculty, the *CD* and the Strike Committee itself.

The first major event of the day was a massive rally in front of the Rotunda, attended by thousands. It was the largest crowd at UVA I had witnessed other than at major sporting events or concerts. A series of speakers addressed the crowd on the evils of the war and the Nixon administration, but there were two speakers in particular that I remember best. The first was Bill Harbaugh, professor of history, who also happened to be my honors history advisor. Bill was a Teddy Roosevelt scholar and was very much dedicated to undergraduate teaching and interacting with students. During the prior year, we had enjoyed many spirited discussions, which were marked by animated repartee and mutual respect. Mr. Harbaugh's indictment of the war was incisive, feisty and witty—which perfectly matched his personality. Right after he finished, one of the more radical members of the Strike Committee took the stage. One of the first things he said was that the forces we should be supporting in Vietnam were not our troops, but rather the NLF (aka, the Vietcong). Well, this did not sit well with me, or for that matter with many others in the crowd, who booed the statement. It was one thing to oppose the war; it was another to support the enemy. That was enough for me, and I departed the gathering for more intelligent and entertaining banter at the AEPi lodge.

*May Days gathering in front of the Rotunda*

Later in the afternoon, another event took place in front of Alderman Library, presumably to hear President Shannon's response to the nine demands presented to him the day before. Those anticipating such response were disappointed, as he did not address in any manner the demands. Rather, he attempted to ameliorate student concerns by announcing that he had spoken to Virginia's two U.S. senators—Harry Byrd and William Spong—and that he had arranged for a group of student leaders to meet with them the following Monday. Mr. Shannon then read from a letter he would be sending the senators confirming the meeting. The letter in part stated that he was "deeply disturbed over the continued alienation of our young men and women owing largely to our nation's military involvement in Southeast Asia" and that it was his "firm conviction that student views and questions on the matter need to be heard by those in position to influence and shape national policy." Having finished reading his letter, President Shannon quickly departed. As he made his way through the crowd, he was greeted by both cheers and jeers, with some of the more exuberant demonstrators tossing marshmallows at him.

I felt a great deal of sympathy for President Shannon at the time.

I knew Edgar Shannon, and he was a fine, compassionate individual who enjoyed interacting with students. The Student Coalition protests in the spring of 1969 and the anti-war activities in the fall had presented him with a number of new scenarios to deal with in terms of student unrest, but nothing had prepared him for the unprecedented turbulence that had descended on the University in May 1970. He was now clearly walking an increasingly fine line between a justifiably concerned student body containing a growing radicalized element and a pro-Nixon Republican governor representing a conservative state that largely disdained student activism. My take on President Shannon was that while he truly empathized with student discontent over the war, he was attempting to avoid having the University become politicized in support of any one side.

After President Shannon left Alderman Library, the crowd began to disperse, with many heading over to University Hall for the Kunstler and Rubin show. To this day, I find it uncanny that Kunstler's and Rubin's appearances at UVA had been planned well before the Cambodia incursion and the resulting turbulence. No one at that time could have imagined that these firebrands would be inserted into a tinderbox of discontent just waiting for the right igniting force. I soon joined the crowds thronging into U Hall, looking forward to what I believed would be a memorable evening. But little did I know how memorable it would be, as one of the most tempestuous events in UVA history was about to unfold.

## Revolution

University Hall was standing room only and the electricity in the building was palpable. As I took my seat, I could see numerous flags waving. Unfortunately, they were Viet Cong flags, not American ones. And as I gazed out on the boisterous denim-and-work-shirt-garbed crowd, with the aroma of weed filtering through the air, I could only marvel at the contrast with the coat-and-tie-bedecked gathering that had filled the same hall at Convocation three-and-a-half years earlier.

Yes indeed, there had been a tidal wave of change in Charlottesville in that short period of time. Another thing I noticed that surprised me was the conspicuous lack of any real security at the event. I did see a number of student "marshals" walking around in their coats and ties, but not much more than that. Maybe the powers-that-be thought that a significant police or security presence would act to instigate the crowd—but as it turned out, "crowd instigation" would be in plentiful supply with or without uniforms present.

*Jerry Rubin and Bill Kunstler—fuel to the fire*

Bill Kunstler took the stage first. In May 1970, Kunstler was one of the most recognizable faces in the country. He had gained his notoriety as defense counsel for the Chicago Seven in a months-long trial emanating from the riots during the 1968 Democratic National Convention. As Kunstler began speaking, it soon became clear that here was a smart, effective rabble-rouser. He called for resistance to the hilt and threatened less than peaceful actions if the resistance was not heeded. What really stuck in my mind were his constant comparisons of the U.S. to Nazi Germany. I found that ironic, as the events going on around me that night specifically brought to mind Leni Riefenstahl's famous propaganda film, Triumph of the Will, about the Nazi Nuremberg rally of 1934. With the flags waving, the crowd being whipped into a frenzy by a charismatic speaker, and the throngs making chopping motions with their arms while screaming "strike, strike" (rather than "heil, heil"), I began to feel chills going up and down my spine. It was sometime during Kunstler's speech that, noticing the crowd reaction, I began to suspect that this was not going to end well.

*Kunstler inciting the crowd*

Once Kunstler finished speaking, Yippie leader Jerry Rubin took center stage. Rubin stood in stark contrast to Kunstler. Kunstler was a serious guy, and all the gravitas that Kunstler encompassed was lacking in Rubin. Rubin was first and foremost a showman, and he pranced around the stage shouting, cajoling and playing to the emotions of the audience. By the time he was done, most of the audience were on their feet yelling and in an excited state. And just as I stood up to leave, someone either on or at the front of the stage screamed "On to Carr's Hill"; and after that came the cry "Burn it down." At that moment, a student marshal who knew me approached me and said, "I think there's going to be trouble. Will you come up with us to Carr's Hill?" So, together with a group of marshals, I sprinted up to Carr's Hill from U Hall (I was in much better shape back then).

For those unfamiliar with the topography of UVA, the president's home on Carr's Hill sits atop a steep incline just northwest of the Rotunda overlooking Fayerweather Hall and Rugby Road to the east and University Avenue to the south. The only direct access is a narrow road off University Avenue and then up a steep series of steps leading to the white columned, two-story, Colonial Revival-style mansion designed by McKim, Mead & White in 1907.

When I finally climbed the steps to the mansion, arriving just below the front porch, I looked around to see how many of us had come to defend the president's home. The answer was, not many. There were perhaps three-dozen of us, but I took some comfort in noting that some of the assembled were varsity athletes, and their presence would help us at least present somewhat of a formidable front. No police or other security officials were in sight. As we stood there trying to come up with some sort of plan, the initial evidence of the approaching masses was discernible. Because of the foliage, we could hear them before we could see them—the shouts of "Strike, strike" and "Burn it down." Then they came into view—there were hundreds, if not thousands, of them snaking up Carr's Hill Road to the mansion. I could see quite a few torches in the crowd as well as numerous open cigarette lighters. I looked back at the president's home and noticed for the first time that most of the windows were dark, with only a few lights on in the mansion. At the time, I remember not knowing whether President Shannon was present, although I had heard that Mrs. Shannon and her five young daughters were at home (I was later informed that President Shannon was at some point in the mansion with Deans Alan Williams and Bob Canevari meeting with a few Student Council and strike leaders).

As the clamorous crowd reached the bottom of the steps, someone in our group shouted something to the effect of "lock arms and form a chain." Which is exactly what we did. We created a human chain in a line across the front entrance of the mansion. I was on one of the wings several yards from the center of the formation, which was lined up with the steps leading to the front porch of the mansion. A few minutes passed, and then the foremost members of the mob reached the top of the steps and stood a few feet in front of us. I don't remember who took the lead in our group, but a discussion then ensued with some of the leaders of the ever-increasing horde of protesters. I could hear bits and pieces of the conversation, and one part I do recall is our spokesman telling the assembled that Mrs. Shannon and her young children were in the house and that the protesters' actions were frightening them—and then politely requesting that they leave. Meanwhile, in the background taunts and threats of forcible entry and conflagration were still being hurled at us, and somewhere in that mass was Bill Kunstler ranting away on a bullhorn and stirring the pot. And so we reached the denouement—we were literally eyeball to eyeball with a frenzied mob that probably outnumbered us by more than twenty-five to one. You could cut the tension with a knife, and I could feel the fellows on either side of me tense as we locked arms even tighter. Then someone at the front of the unruly throng yelled "On to Maury Hall," and the mob turned around and headed off for easier pickings. As the masses departed, my colleagues and I exhaled as one. And thus ended the "Siege of Carr's Hill."

I am normally not one given to hyperbole, and while the defense of Carr's Hill was not exactly the 300 Spartans at Thermopylae or the "Thin Red Line" of the 93rd Highlanders at Balaclava,[55] it was, as the Duke of Wellington said after the Battle of Waterloo, "A damn close-run thing." I truly believe that we were only moments away from violent confrontation that evening. There were many outside agitators and

---

55   During the Persian second invasion of Greece in 480 BC, a small rearguard of Greek warriors led by King Leonidas of Sparta and his 300 Spartans held off tens of thousands of invading Persians for a week at the narrow coastal pass of Thermopylae before being totally annihilated. The 93rd Highlanders fared much better against a massive charge of Russian cavalry at the Battle of Balaclava during the Crimean War in 1854. Famed *London Times* reporter William H. Russell wrote that the only thing to be seen between the charging Russian cavalry and the British base of operations at Balaclava was the 93rd Highlanders "thin red streak tipped with a line of steel." This "thin red line" only two men deep routed the Russian cavalry. Later that same day would occur the even more famous Charge of the Light Brigade.

radicals in that crowd, and no one knows how badly this might have ended. I do know that I was physically and emotionally exhausted after the confrontation and quickly departed to the Crackerbox for a well-earned night's repose.

As time goes by, many of us wonder whether stories from the past become embellished and dramatized. It's only human to do so. But my memories of that evening are vivid, and several years ago they received validation from an unexpected source. I was at a dinner at the University honoring undergraduate research. Seated next to me was a professor who had first arrived at UVA in the mid 1970s. He asked me what the University was like prior to his arrival. I told him some stories, including the march on Carr's Hill. About a week later, I received an email from him saying that he had coincidentally bumped into Alan Williams and he had asked Mr. Williams whether he remembered me. He wrote that Alan responded by saying, "Sure, I remember Joel. Ask him if he still has the bruises on his arms from forming the chain defending Carr's Hill." So I guess my memory still serves me fairly well.

Since I retired to the Crackerbox soon after the events described above, it was not until the following morning that I learned what had transpired at Maury Hall after the agitators left Carr's Hill. Much, if not most, of the crowd that had descended on Carr's Hill marched over to Maury Hall where approximately two hundred of the group occupied that building for a second time. There were a number of student marshals who tried to keep the occupiers in the second-floor auditorium, but soon the demonstrators were all over the building. It was then already past midnight.

At about 1:40 a.m., Student Council member Kevin Mannix, who had previously been meeting with President Shannon, announced to the occupiers that they were to evacuate the building immediately, as they were in violation of the previously issued court injunction. Meanwhile, some provocateurs had apparently tried to set Maury Hall on fire, as a smoldering mattress and other burnt materials were discovered in the basement. The discovery of the burning mattress combined with the belief that the police would soon be coming to enforce the injunction resulted in the abandonment of the building by the occupiers. This marked the final act in what was one of the most explosive and intense days in UVA's history.

Wednesday night's events would have an immediate impact on the atmosphere on Grounds. First, the administration apparently finally recognized the real danger of violence emanating from the strike activities. As noted previously, I had been surprised by the lack of police presence at U Hall Wednesday night and even more so by their absence at Carr's Hill afterwards. Given the initial Maury Hall takeover Monday night, the prior march on Carr's Hill, and the increasing presence of outsiders at protest events, it was astonishing to me that the administration had not significantly increased security on Grounds. This was now remedied, and one could readily notice an increased police presence at strike activities—a reality that would play a major role in the next memorable event of May 1970.

*The smoldering remnants of the attempt to ignite Maury Hall*

An additional major ramification of Wednesday night's episodes was the recognition by many members of the University community that the protests were out of control and that many of the strike participants were not interested in reasoned or reasonable discourse. *The Cavalier Daily*, which had previously supported most of the aims of the strike, issued a scathing indictment of the strike leadership, or lack thereof:

> It was all bound to end up this way. At least it was since the strike from the beginning lacked both leadership and reason. The movement which was sparked by President Nixon's inexcusable decision to escalate the war in Indochina had many important substantive issues, but at the University it has become polluted with ineffectual and irresponsible leaders and numbers of people from outside the University community who would just as soon see the Grounds burned as left intact. What we have witnessed in the past few days is the arrival on Grounds of the very evils against which the strikers preach. Totalitarianism and repression now characterize the activities of the strike as witnessed by the marches on Carr's Hill and Maury Hall.
>
> -----
>
> The radicals and their unthinking followers now chant to 'shut down' and to 'burn it,' losing all perspective of the conditions in this country which started all of the sensible and indeed necessary activities of the beginning of the week.
>
> -----
>
> The whole strike has suffered from a serious vacuum of leadership which has resulted in unproductive and clearly avoidable confrontation. What began as a

movement by the whole University has become a strike against the University which ultimately will serve no purpose and has already resulted in foolish violence.

So the violent actions of Wednesday night cost the strike the support of many moderate and progressive students who otherwise backed many or some of its goals. These students realized that the radical agenda of many of the strikers was not their agenda. What was missing were those basic elements of civil discourse and free and open debate— respect for your opponent's point of view and a willingness to compromise.

In view of the above, many of the strike leaders sought to reconsider their strategy as dawn broke on Thursday. They met with their supporters on the Lawn to assess the damage done to the cause by the violence the night before. To many, the extreme actions on Wednesday night all but killed the strike. King Golden, the Law School President-elect and a strike supporter, told the assembled that the strike should be discontinued if "it is continued to be led by those who have no concern for student moderates or libertarian ideals." And my erstwhile friend Bruce Wine addressing the crowd admitted that "We blew it" by losing sight of the goals the strike leaders had set for themselves. In the end, the more moderate strike leaders prevailed, and a decision was made to hold a referendum the following Monday on the strike and the nine demands previously presented to President Shannon. In the meantime, there was agreement to continue the strike for the rest of the week.

As a student of Russian history and an astute observer of what was happening in real time with the strike movement, it seemed to me that it was a tussle akin to the ideological one among Bakunin, Lenin, and Kerensky.[56] Should they burn the U down, shut it down by force or shut it down by parliamentary procedure? In my mind, shutting the

---

56  Mikhail Bakunin was a Russian revolutionary and leading anarchist; Vladimir Lenin was the leader of the Bolshevik faction of the Russian revolutionaries; and Alexander Kerensky was the moderate leader of the Social Revolutionaries and the Prime Minister of the Provisional Government at the time of the Bolshevik Revolution.

University down by any means was wrong. Demonstrate and protest all you want—UVA, like any university, should be a forum for the free exchange of all kinds of points of view. But there was nothing libertarian or Jeffersonian in dictating whether or not I could or couldn't attend classes and further my intellectual boundaries. I agreed with President Shannon that UVA should not be used as a weapon to further any political agenda. Not that my viewpoint was worth a hill of beans to the strikers at that moment. Most of those members of the UVA community who agreed with me, and I would venture to say that it was at least half, were not participating in strike activities, and were either observing with interest, observing with mild amusement as the strike leaders bickered and fought amongst themselves, or, like Rhett Butler, frankly didn't give a damn.

In any event, Thursday passed without further disruptive activities, until an incident occurred that evening that would be a harbinger of the debacle that would follow the next day. A crowd of individuals had begun a demonstration just north of the Rotunda, near the intersection of University Avenue and Rugby Road, displaying signs to motorists saying, "Honk for Peace." As the number of demonstrators grew to over a hundred, they moved down University Avenue and congregated at the intersection of Emmet Street (Route 29) and Ivy Road (Route 250) by the Downtowner Motor Inn (later the Cavalier Inn). The "honk-in" continued, causing a traffic snarl at the intersection, and it did not take long for the newly increased police presence to assert itself. About forty policemen arrived at the scene and caused the demonstrators to retreat south on Emmet Street beyond Memorial Gym, where they took up a position on the hillside overlooking the road. There then ensued a face-off between the demonstrators and the police. Deans Alan Williams and Bob Canevari soon arrived on the scene and in sequence convinced the police to back off from the confrontation and the demonstrators to disperse. Unfortunately, a similar confrontation the next night would not have such a peaceful ending.

Friday, May 8, unfolded in a remarkably similar manner to the day before. It was relatively peaceful during the day, but as evening arrived crowds again began to form for a "honk-in" in front of the Rotunda. As was the case on Thursday, the demonstrators then moved down toward the Downtowner, where the honk-in continued. However, this time when confronted by the police, the crowd moved back toward their original position in front of the Rotunda rather than south on Emmet Street. While this was unfolding, I was on the way back to the Crackerbox after dining at the Pi house and participating in the usual after-dinner repartee. I can remember driving down Rugby Road and seeing crowds forming in front of the Rotunda. Heaving heard what had transpired the night before, I figured this would be a repeat performance. So I went home to the Crackerbox to continue preparing for my oral and written honors exams. While at that point it was becoming increasingly clear that many professors either would not be holding final exams or would be giving them on an optional basis, my honors program was the culmination of two years of work, and it had been made clear that students who wanted their honors degree would have to take the exams.

When I arrived at the Crackerbox, it was empty, so I figured that Steve Hayes might well be out enjoying the spectacle of the honk-in. It was a lovely spring Friday night, and at that point the demonstrations had become something of a spectator sport for many students. It was about an hour later when the door suddenly flew open. Hayes rushed into the room, slammed the door shut, locked it and turned out the lights. In response to my "What the hell?" he said, "They're after me"— of course raising the questions who "they" were and why.

Steve then related to me the events of the evening. As I had surmised, he had moseyed over to the Rotunda to witness the evening's activities. The honk-in protestors had just arrived back there after having been confronted at the Downtowner and, as the protesters were combined with hundreds of spectators, another traffic snarl developed on University Avenue. It did not take long for a police contingent to assemble to confront the gathered masses. Steve and most of the other spectators, as well as most of the demonstrators, were on the south side of University Avenue in front of the Rotunda. The police, in full riot gear, gathered in a solid line across the avenue in front of Madison Hall, facing the crowd across the road. Dean Williams was on a megaphone shouting something undecipherable to the demonstrators. After Williams stopped speaking there was a lull, and then suddenly, for no apparent reason, the line of police adorned with helmets and batons charged across the street.

In response to this immediate threat, Steve and scores of other spectators and demonstrators did an about-face and hightailed it up the hill toward the Lawn with the police in hot pursuit. The fleeing crowd thought the "sacred" confines of the Lawn would be a sanctuary from police incursion—but they were sadly mistaken. The police proceeded to enter Mr. Jefferson's village and charge down the Lawn, grabbing students willy-nilly along the way and even plucking some from Lawn rooms where they had been seeking refuge. Fortunately for Hayes, he was a speedy runner (he would later break the two-mile run record at Fort Benning) and he was able to make it unscathed to the steps at the southeast end of the Lawn leading down to Randall Hall and the safety of the Crackerbox. I remember being astonished by his story, and we kept the lights out in the Crackerbox for the rest of the night and did not emerge until the following morning, when we learned the full extent of the prior night's debacle.

The unprecedented police action on Friday night would quickly have major repercussions. First, the details. Sixty-eight people were arrested that evening and unceremoniously carted away in a Mayflower moving van that had been parked nearby waiting for such an incident. Astoundingly, a good number of those arrested were not protesters but rather observers or folks who had just happened to be in the wrong place at the wrong time. The police had not just charged down the Lawn, they had also invaded Rugby Road and Mad Lane, arresting unsuspecting students and their dates and even dragging some out of the fraternity houses.

Perhaps the most outrageous incident of an evening filled with many involved the arrests of a number of the members of the KA house. Now, back then, one could not find a more Southern and Old U fraternity than KA. And appropriately, that weekend the KAs were having their black tie Convivium celebration in honor of Robert E. Lee. Well, that Friday night several of the penguin-suited KAs and their dates strolled down Rugby Road from Grady Avenue, interested in the events transpiring in front of the Rotunda. As noted, the police were fairly indiscriminate in their arrests once unleashed, and in their enthusiasm corralled a number of KAs, including my good friend Tom Sansonetti. Tom, who would later become the Chairman of the Wyoming Republican Party and serve as an Assistant U.S. Attorney General under Bush II, was hardly the radical protester that one would expect to find in the back of a police paddy wagon. Indeed, Tom subsequently prevailed before the city court judge, when the judge refused to believe that a fellow in a tuxedo was guilty of "inciting to riot."

*Nattily attired denizens of Rugby Road approaching the Rotunda*
*moments before all hell breaks loose*

The gross overreaction of the police on Friday night caused the pendulum of student opinion to swing back in favor of the strike and against the establishment. The Strike Committee, which had been dealt a severe blow by the excesses exhibited a few nights earlier at Carr's Hill and Maury Hall, was now in ascendancy again. As an example, the *CD* editorial staff, which had just recently condemned the actions of many of the protesters, now turned its ire on the police and the University administration. In an emotional editorial entitled "The Pigs," the *CD* asserted that "We have nothing but contempt for the state, city and county police" and that "to call the officers of the law pigs is perhaps too mild." Noting that "President Shannon should never have turned control of the situation over to the police," the editorial concluded, "The small group of students who wanted a confrontation with the police before Friday night has now expanded as a result of the invasion of the Grounds. Many students want to show the pigs that they consider themselves above their authority." So the protest movement was back in business.

*Mr. Jefferson's serpentine walls are not immune to the strike*

The culmination of what would subsequently be referred to by many as the "May Days" occurred on a sunny Sunday afternoon on May 10, 1970. I remember it being the largest outdoor gathering of this incredible week, as President Shannon addressed a crowd later estimated to be four thousand strong. As Mr. Shannon continued to attempt to walk a political tightrope, he was sequentially and repeatedly booed and applauded. On the one hand, he took his strongest stand against the war, calling for prompt action to end it. He read from a letter he had drafted to Virginia's two U.S. senators, in which he asserted he was "gravely concerned by many instances of anti-intellectualism and growing militarism in the national government of the United States" and by the "verbal attacks upon universities, students, and the free press by persons in the highest levels of government."[57] President Shannon then called on Byrd and Spong to "join with your fellow Senators in reasserting the authority of the Senate over the foreign policy of the United States and the use of the armed forces in its support."

On the other hand, President Shannon also recounted the disturbances of the prior week and referred to the demonstrators who marched on Carr's Hill and occupied Maury Hall as "mobs." These comments provoked many catcalls and hisses from the crowd. But the statement I remember most that afternoon was at the beginning of his speech, when President Shannon stated that to his knowledge UVA was the only major university on the East Coast that was still open. I didn't know for sure then if we truly stood alone, and still don't know if that was true at the time. But it was a powerful statement, and I believed then and believe now that UVA keeping its doors open was a real tribute to the University's students, faculty and administration.

President Shannon's May 10 speech was the last major event of May Days, although strike-related activities would continue in one form or

---

57 Here is another example of the themes of that time resonating strongly with the current climate in our nation. That part of the letter could be written verbatim today by certain political leaders.

another for a few more weeks. Not surprisingly, the following day the student body voted two to one to continue the strike. However, at the same time they also voted overwhelmingly to reject three of the nine demands made by the Strike Committee—those dealing with removing ROTC from Grounds, severing ties with the JAG School, and terminating research relating to the Defense Department—once again demonstrating the common sense of your average Wahoo.

*President Shannon addressing mass rally on the Lawn*

Anyway, what did continuing the strike really mean? The University was still "open," classes were still being held and the semester was just about over. In actuality, the continuation of the strike took on a particularly UVA character. Those who wanted to participate in strike activities were generally encouraged to do so and those who wanted to continue with their education were allowed to do so. In furtherance of this broad compromise, a committee of the heads of the departments of the College recommended three alternatives to the faculty on how to deal with the question of final exams: 1) postpone the final exam until fall 1970 semester; 2) use course averages as of May 1 as a final grade; or 3) construct an alternative work assignment to be completed by June 3. It is important to note that these were recommendations only, and faculty members were free to pursue the course they deemed appropriate—although the pressure was great not to make final exams mandatory.

As noted earlier, none of this affected me, as I was arduously preparing for my honors exams. However, I do remember many students not particularly enamored with the strike still voting for it anyway, so that they could "punt" finals and spend these last few beautiful spring days of the semester either going down the road or getting to know better the numerous women from the surrounding schools that had flooded Grounds to partake in the strike activities. So for many, the following few weeks took on a quasi-party atmosphere—there were impromptu concerts, Frisbees flying through the air, and the pervasive odor of hooch filtering through the Grounds. Yes, there were serious strikers who used the time to continue protesting and to travel to Washington, D.C., and other venues to advance the cause. But my recollection is that things were much more mellow after the Friday night police showdown and President Shannon's speech on Sunday. The "honk-in" devotees showed up again on Monday night, but they did not impede traffic and there were no confrontations. After that, it was fairly quiet as underclassmen without exams started to drift home and fourth-year men prepared for graduation.

So, what was the legacy of May Days? There were a number of immediate ramifications. First, as noted above, the spring semester was truncated. For all intents and purposes, the semester was over after President Shannon's speech and the approval by most faculty of a flexible or no-exam policy. Second, the Class of 1970's graduation ceremonies became somewhat anticlimactic. The class parties and celebrations that usually preceded graduation were lost in the strike's aftermath. Our Class President, Pete Schmidt, tried to form a consensus as to celebratory functions and our class gift, but was met at every turn by dissension and controversy. A class referendum was announced and then cancelled. In the end, I don't remember attending any class celebrations. For many, it was a disappointing end of our four years at UVA.

Another immediate result of May Days was the widespread criticism directed at President Shannon and the University from various quarters in the Commonwealth. As Virginia has recently turned from a "red" to a "purple" to a "blue" state, it is once again significant to place in context the student demonstrations in a deeply conservative Old Dominion. Republican Governor Linwood Holton quickly made it clear that he disagreed with President Shannon's statement on the war. He further called for an end to the strike and advised the students to "go back to the classes, to go back to the books." The governor referred to the many letters and telegrams he received that were critical of Shannon and the University and stated that "the taxpayers are now mad and are ready to cut off money that supports higher education." The Commonwealth's leading newspaper, the *Richmond Times-Dispatch*, severely criticized President Shannon for "practicing appeasement" toward the protesters and for negotiating with them "under conditions of duress." It also excoriated him for having caved in to "the irresponsible radicals on his campus [sic]" by issuing a "maliciously warped letter" to Virginia's senators.

In addition, President Shannon was also rebuked by members of his own faculty at a time when there was a material diversity of ideology in that sector. One of them, Associate Professor William Breit of the economics department, penned an open letter to *The Cavalier Daily* in which he asserted that Mr. Shannon's statement on the war and his suggestion that the faculty should allow flexibility in fulfilling academic requirements "has moved this University toward the day when it will be destroyed as the home of free enquiry and the uninhibited search for the truth" because he had taken a political position on behalf of the institution he represented. According to the professor, Shannon's actions had made "the University an instrument of oppression against the individual professor or student who disagrees with [his] views on these issues." As a libertarian, I saw much merit in Mr. Breit's views, but as a pragmatist as well, I sympathized with President Shannon's attempts to keep the University open, avoid violence, and express empathy with numerous conflicting constituencies. And in my mind, he had done about as good a job of achieving these goals as was possible under these incredibly troublesome and unprecedented circumstances.

Based on subsequent discussions I had with President Shannon and others who knew him well, these two weeks were exceptionally difficult for him, and in the end defined his fifteen-year term as President of the University. This was unfortunate—in that for many he would not be remembered for his intelligent and measured shepherding of the University into a new era, but rather for a few weeks' period, where most thought that he had either done too much or had not done enough.

As for the longer-term consequences of the May Days, the anti-war demonstrations and activities at UVA and other campuses had little effect on national policy. The war would go on for another five years; and in 1972, in one of the greatest landslide victories in U.S. history, Dick Nixon would be reelected over George McGovern, who had likewise called for an immediate withdrawal of our troops from Vietnam.

*With [L-R] Jim Roebuck, President Shannon, and Bruce Wine on a panel discussing "May Days" at my 25th Reunion*

Similarly, there were few direct long-term consequences at UVA. While I was not in Charlottesville for the following school year, 1970-1971, I understand that it was a relatively quiet year. And for the three years I was in law school, even though the war was still raging, there were no major disturbances, and ROTC and the JAG school still thrived on Grounds. Perhaps the bulk of the underclassmen who had witnessed the events of May 1970 had decided that unbridled agitation and a failure to respect others' points of view were not the road to travel to achieve one's objectives. In fact, it is probably safe to say that in the almost fifty years since those events, nothing has ever approached the turbulence and tumult that we witnessed in the spring of 1970.

Nevertheless, while there have not been disturbances or agitation to match that of May Days, the spirit of that period has reemerged on Grounds in recent years with a heady brew of social and political agendas, accompanied by a strong dash of moral superiority, and with a sprinkling of intolerance for opposing viewpoints. This was most glaringly evident during the Rolling Stone fiasco in late 2015, when members of the faculty led demonstrations against their own students in a Salem-witch-hunt-like atmosphere and the rights of groups of students were sacrificed on the altar of political correctness.[58] While UVA has not approached the level of such behavior as witnessed at schools such as Michigan, Wisconsin, Yale, or Berkeley, it is apparent that the seeds for such conduct have been sown in fertile soil.

---

58  I am also sorry to have to report that as I was putting the finishing touches on this story, I read in *The Cavalier Daily* that one of the candidates in the spring 2017 Student Council presidential election was the subject of numerous ad hominem attacks. As an avid reader of the *CD* for decades, I couldn't remember seeing anything quite as nasty as that since my era. It really does seem that the excesses of that period are back in vogue. And I could feel that candidate's pain, remembering the deep disappointment I felt that something like that could happen at UVA. And even more recently, as I was submitting this manuscript for publication in the fall of 2017, it was reported that an activist group of students had invaded the St. Anthony Hall fraternity house in an attempt to prevent a private party from occurring. This represented the first time to my knowledge that one group of UVA students trespassed on the private property of another group of UVA students to forcibly disrupt a private social event. The University administration had no official comment.

Thus, although one might find it difficult to point to a specific legacy of the events of May 1970, it did in fact serve as a fitting bookend to my four years as an undergraduate. When I counterpose sitting in my coat and tie listening to Braxton Woody's honor address with standing in front of Carr's Hill facing the hordes demanding to burn it down, I can only be astonished at the transformation that had turned the world in Charlottesville upside down. If it had not been clear before, it was now indisputable that the Old U was gone and never to return.

And yet, even today one can find remnants of the Old U in life at UVA. Foremost is the central place that the Honor System still holds at the University. Sure, it has changed to reflect the mores of the current student body, which has left the system a shadow of its former self. But in a collegiate world of dubious traditional values, the fact that it still exists even in its diluted form is a credit to the enduring spirit of honor at the U. And I daresay that most current Wahoos still could not imagine UVA being UVA without it. The vestiges of the coat-and-tie ethos can still be witnessed on a fine fall day at a football game, where bow ties and sundresses are in full bloom at Scott Stadium. The Elis and T.I.L.K.A.s still march (although many students no longer know who or what they are) and the Z, IMP, and Seven symbols are still very visible on Grounds.

But mostly the Old U lives on in the character and sociability of the students that emerge from the Grounds after four years in Charlottesville. Collegiality and integrity are still hallmarks of your typical Wahoo. In the forty years I was a professional and was very active in recruiting for my respective firms, I noticed a consistently strong inclination to hire UVA students. In addition to being smart and talented, Wahoos tend to be reliable team players who are pleasant and interesting to be around. Some things just don't change.

## *What a Long Strange Trip It's Been*[59]

It was Saturday night, June 6, 1970, the day before graduation. I had been to dinner with my parents and my brother and returned to the Crackerbox. Hayes was still out with his family, so I strolled up to the Lawn. I quickly ran into my fraternity brother, Al Margulies, who resided on the West Lawn, accompanied by fellow brother, Bill "Choo Choo" Brener. Margulies and Brener both stood in the top five academically in our class, were two of the brightest people I have ever met and would both go on to become eminent physicians in their respective fields. We chatted for a while, reminiscing about our years together at the U and our future plans. When we were done, it was almost midnight, and the Lawn was virtually deserted. Instead of returning to the Crackerbox, I climbed up the steps to the Rotunda and plunked myself down on the top step, looking out over Mr. Jefferson's masterpiece. Not a sound was to be heard or a person to be seen. It is still astonishing to me today that at night you can be on the Lawn, the center of a university with over twenty thousand students, and feel as if you are the only person in town.

So there I was, alone with my thoughts. And it all came back to me in a rush. What an amazing four years I had experienced. How much I had changed as a person. The incredible people I had met. The astounding transformation that had taken place around me. Mostly I focused on my journey—and what a lucky fellow I was. How this son of an immigrant who had come to this country in steerage had arrived at this bastion of Southern gentility knowing no one, and yet four years later had felt so at home and so fulfilled. I thought about the greatness of our country and the validity of the "melting pot." And looking out at the beauty of the pavilions and the colonnades, I thought about how this great institution had opened its arms to this stranger and had embraced me with its history, traditions and values. And I remembered the poem that I had read just days before for the first time—"The Honor Men," written by James Hay Jr. in 1903—certain verses of which kept coming back to me:

---

59  With compliments to Robert Hunter and the Grateful Dead ("Truckin," 1970)

if you live a long long time,
and hold honesty of conscience
above honesty of purse; and turn
aside without ostentation to aid
the weak; and treasure ideals
more than raw ambition; and
track no man to his undeserved
hurt; and pursue no woman to her
tears; and love the beauty of noble
music and mist-veiled mountains
and blossoming valleys and great
monuments—

-----

Then…remembering the purple
shadows of the lawn, the majesty
of the colonnades, and the dream
of your youth, you may say in
reverence and thankfulness:
"I have worn the honors of honor,
I graduated from Virginia".

And as tears welled in my eyes (as they still do today when I read that poem) I knew then and there that the University would always be part of who I am, and that no matter where I was, part of me would always be in Charlottesville. But my sadness at leaving the Grounds after graduation was somewhat abated by the knowledge that I would be returning to the University for law school, and thus that my journey would continue.

# EPILOGUE

After graduating, I still did not know when I was going to be called for active duty, so I returned for another summer of fun and games with my buddies as a group leader at camp. The summer over, and still no notice from Uncle Sam, I headed out on a journey to see America by camping out cross country with my camp friend, Jeff Sultan. We made it through the Badlands, the Black Mountains, Yellowstone, the Grand Tetons, and Yosemite, and I was settling in for dinner around the campfire in Sequoia National Park in mid-October when Jeff came back with a smile on his face after calling his folks from the park ranger's outpost. I can still remember those words—you have ten days to report to Fort Dix. So we packed up our gear, drove to Los Angeles, sold our car, and flew back to New York.

Two weeks later, I was doing hundred-yard low crawls, tossing grenades, and bayoneting targets. What helped me get through those days of basic training and then advanced training at Fort Devens was the knowledge that I would finish active duty by the summer of 1971, and thus would be able to be back in Charlottesville for law school for the 1971-1972 school year.

My law school experience at UVA was almost as rewarding as my undergraduate days. I was in the last class to graduate from Clark Hall before the Law School moved to North Grounds.[60] So I was still only steps away from the Lawn on a daily basis, and back then, law students felt much more a part of the University as a whole. I have always believed that both the University and the students lost out big-

---

60 The North Grounds is a complex initially constructed in 1974 to house new law school and graduate business school structures. It is about one mile north of Central Grounds.

time when the Law School moved away from Central Grounds. I was also fortunate to have in my class three of my closest friends—Steve Brickman, Whitt Clement, and Bill Fryer—as well as four additional fraternity brothers.

First year of law school was probably the most valuable academic year of my university career—the Socratic method and all that. They actually did teach one how to approach various issues in a logical manner, a discipline that would be valuable in many situations beyond the law. Being back in Charlottesville in 1971 was also my introduction to the benefits of coeducation. And I can remember asking myself over and over again—"What was I thinking…?"

After focusing on studies almost exclusively first year, I returned to pursuing extracurricular and journalistic activities outside the classroom my second year. So in addition to keeping up with classes, I was busy on the Editorial Board of the *Virginia Law Review*, was elected to Student Council, where I served with future UVA legend and political pundit Larry Sabato, and, perhaps most enjoyable to me, I became the Guru of the T.I.L.K.A.s. I don't think I ever got more than five hours of sleep a night that year.

Since I already had a job offer after having been a summer associate at a major Wall Street law firm, third year of law school was relatively relaxing and anticlimactic, and in my view, pretty much extraneous. In any event, it was a bittersweet year, knowing that it would be my last as a student at the University.

After receiving my law degree, I returned to NYC, where I began the practice of law at Davis Polk & Wardwell and then segued into the investment banking world of mergers and acquisitions. Although I was firmly ensconced in the Big Apple, the University was never far away. I was surrounded by UVA friends and usually made a few trips a year to Charlottesville to interview students for my firm or to attend football games.

When the University became serious about fundraising after John Casteen became president in 1990, I quickly got involved in development activities. I was a founding board member of the Rotunda Society, served as Vice-Chair of the Annual Giving Advisory Board, was a member of the Benefactors Society Board for the College and twice was gift chair for the Class of 1970 reunions. Most recently I have become a board member of the Jefferson Grounds Initiative. My wife, Gayle, has made it a family affair by serving on the University Arts Council. And I was also proud to become a University parent when our daughter, Allie, attended the University.

Finally, I have come full circle by returning to my "spiritual" home after four decades in New York. My wife and I now split our time between Charlottesville and Florida. We exchanged our view of the Empire State Building for views of the Blue Ridge Mountains and the Atlantic Ocean—more than a fair trade in my mind.

*With Steve Brickman (L) and Whitt Clement (R) in law school*

Some of my friends have suggested that I returned to Charlottesville and am writing this book in an attempt to turn back the clock and return to the days of my youth. Nothing could be further from the truth. Because in actuality, I never left the University, and as my wife will attest, I never really left my youth. Many Wahoos depart Charlottesville, look back fondly, and don't give much thought to UVA, instead focusing on many other parts of their expanding life experiences. For me, the University has been ever present in my existence. I have never viewed life as a series of closing chapters. Rather I see it as a continuum—past, present, future, each playing an active role in who you are and what you do. And in my life, my experiences at the University have been a material part of that continuum.

In closing, my fervent wish is that this book will in some way inspire Wahoos past, present, and future to take part in ensuring that future generations have an opportunity to walk Mr. Jefferson's Grounds, be thrilled by the majesty of the Lawn, and partake in a unique and exceptional culture that has captivated the hearts of so many that have been fortunate to "have worn the honors of honor."

WAHOO-WAH.

# About the Author

Joel Gardner was born and raised in New York City. He graduated from the University of Virginia with an Honors Degree in History in 1970 and from its School of Law in 1974, where he was a member of the *Law Review*. He returned to NYC to practice law at a major Wall Street firm and subsequently entered the investment banking world, where he was an M&A banker for three decades specializing in transactions involving Asian-based companies. Gardner has been actively involved with the University of Virginia in numerous capacities since his graduation, and he and his wife Gayle now split their time between Charlottesville and Boca Raton, Florida.

# Photo Credits

Page 30: The flaming Z (*Corks and Curls*)

Page 32: Hey! Hey! Hey! T-I-L-K-A (*Corks and Curls*)

Page 32: The Elis marching (*Corks and Curls*)

Page 34: Coronation of King IMP Pete Gray (*Corks and Curls*)

Page 40: The Deans *(Corks and Curls)*

Page 43: The timeless Lawn (*Corks and Curls*)

Page 56: Frank Quayle busting through *(Corks and Curls)*

Page 66: Front page of The Cavalier Daily, Openings 1966 (*The Cavalier Daily*)

Page 71: Big weekend party at the AEPi house 1966 (*Corks and Curls*)

Page 72: The detritus of a big weekend party (*Corks and Curls*)

Page 76: Dean B.F.D. Runk (*Corks and Curls*)

Page 81: AEPi house in 1966 (*Corks and Curls*)

Page 84: The AEPi family in 1969 *(Corks and Curls)*

Page 107: What were they thinking? (*The Cavalier Daily*)

Page 118: The Anarchists arise (*The Cavalier Daily*)

Page 132: The last mile of the Olympic torch 'marathon' (*The Cavalier Daily*)

Page 134: Attending Mr. Kett's honor seminar […] *(The Cavalier Daily)*

Page 146: […] the Lawn Student Coalition rally (*The Cavalier Daily*)

Page 148: President and Mrs. Shannon at Carr's Hill (*Corks and Curls*)

Page 187: Founding Fathers of the Jefferson Party *(Corks and Curls)*

Page 201: May Days gathering in front of the Rotunda (*UVA Special Collections*)

Page 203: Jerry Rubin and Bill Kunstler – fuel to the fire (*UVA Special Collections*)

Page 204: Kunstler inciting the crowd (*UVA Special Collections*)

Page 208: The smoldering remnants […] (*UVA Special Collections*)

Page 214: […] moments before all hell breaks loose (*UVA Special Collections*)

Page 215: Mr. Jefferson's serpentine walls […] (*UVA Special Collections*)

Page 217: President Shannon addressing mass rally […] (*UVA Special Collections*)